ALCHEMY OF THE HEART

The Healing Journey From Heartbreak to Wholeness

A. Marina Aguilar

CHIRON PUBLICATIONS • ASHEVILLE, NORTH CAROLINA

www.ChironPublications.com

Interior and cover design by Daliborka Mijailović
Printed primarily in the United States of America.

ISBN 978-1-63051-450-1 paperback
ISBN 978-1-63051-451-8 hardcover
ISBN 978-1-63051-452-5 electronic
ISBN 978-1-63051-453-2 limited edition paperback

Library of Congress Cataloging-in-Publication Data

Names: Aguilar, A. Marina, author.
Title: Alchemy of the heart : the sacred marriage of Dionysos & Ariadne / A. Marina Aguilar.
Description: Asheville : Chiron Publications, 2018. | Includes bibliographical references and index.
Identifiers: LCCN 2017055504| ISBN 9781630514501 (pbk. : alk. paper) | ISBN 9781630514518 (hardcover : alk. paper)
Subjects: LCSH: Ariadne (Greek mythology) | Dionysus (Greek deity)
Classification: LCC BL820.A83 A68 2018 | DDC 292.2/11--dc23
LC record available at https://lccn.loc.gov/2017055504

Permissions:
Images from The Alchemical Tarot, Renewed, Fourth Edition; copyright Robert M. Place 2015. http://robertmplacetarot.com, http://burningserpent.com
Map of ancient Greece and Asia Minor. Drawn for this publication by William L. Nelson.
Color plates are reproduced by permission of Scala/Art Resource. N.Y.
The Frescoes in the Initiation Chamber, The Villa dei Misteri, Pompeii

For my children, Alessandro, Arielle and Daniel.
You are exquisite, precious, unique, and brilliant,
each in your own fashion... and you are the light of my life.

In loving memory of Margot, Antonio, Robert and Maud.

With boundless thanks to Maria Starr, Lorraine Geiger, Yolanda Valenzuela, and John Petz for the great gift of your time and care in the preparation of this project.

Special thanks to Laurel Airica, editor and wordsmith par excellence, who deftly helped organize and launch this project.

Thank you to Rabbi Mel Gottlieb and Dr. Paul Clark for mentoring me on the initiatory journey of Kabbalah and Spiritual Alchemy.

Thank you to psychotherapist Bob Hyman, a true master of the craft, who taught me so much by his counseling supervision and his example.

Thank you to Leigh and Carla McCloskey, who inspire so many as healthy present-day embodiments of Dionysos and Ariadne.

Thank you to Pacifica Graduate Institute for providing me with an excellent education, and for the privilege of studying with such extraordinary analysts, teachers, and scholars in the field of depth psychology.

Finally, with deep respect and endless gratitude to my clients, who have trusted me to accompany them as they made their way through the twists and turns of their souls' path. I have learned and grown so much from you.

CONTENTS

PART ONE
HISTORY: ORIGINS, MYTHS AND MYSTERIES

Contents

PART THREE
DIONYSOS AND ARIADNE IN TODAY'S WORLD

Ivy hair,
  ear splitting,
   Dionysos
is who I am going to sing about,
the great son,
  of the glorious goddess,
   Semele,
and of Zeus;
the nymphs,
  with lovely hair,
   took him
from the hands of his lord father Zeus
to their bosoms
  and carefully,
   carefully
nourished him in the caves of Mount Nysa.
He grew,
  with the help of his father,
   among non-mortals
in the wonderful smells of that cave.
Then he started
  dashing
   all over the woods and valleys
when the goddesses were finished with him,
when, with ivy,
  with laurel,
   he was now decorated
and sung about, how, so often.
And the nymphs
  came too, dashing,
   he led them,
the whole forest possessed by their noise.

Alchemy of the Heart

Oh Dionysos,
> *with all your grapes,*
> > *farewell:*
But make it possible
> *for us to come back again*
> *to this happy season—*
> *and after that season,*
> *on into many years.*
> — Second Hymn to Dionysos, *The Homeric Hymns*

Introduction

Dionysos and the Healing of the Heart

This book began as a reflection of a personal journey of transformation with broader implications. As a young woman, I experienced the shattering of romantic illusion. Through its loss, and struggling through the defenses and distortions that wounding brings initially, a deeper and higher understanding and experience has emerged and changed me. This has been my personal Individuation journey; and, through my work with female clients for nearly thirty years, I know that it is the soul task of many women.[1] The instinctive projection of completion and redemption onto a human lover can and should be deepened and transmuted into a marriage of the feminine soul with the hidden "other" within the psyche. Maturity and wholeness are its fruit.

As the Chinese Yin/Yang symbol so clearly depicts, within each of us lies the seed of the other. The goal of this spiritual and psychological inner partnership is referred to as the *Sacred Marriage* in myth and mystical religion. It is a spiritual tantra of the union of the opposites in the psyche. The outer lover points the way to the inner sustaining Lover. This realization brings meaning and purpose to our heartbreaks… in fact, breaking the heart open to a wider and deeper love. This journey knows suffering and expands the heart in compassion for the pathos of the world, and its personal gift is the soul's fulfillment and completion. Rather than separate and alienate a woman

---

[1] *Individuation* in Jungian terminology refers to the evolution towards wholeness and full flowering of one's psychological potential. It is never complete but is an ever-evolving, ongoing process.

from others, it makes her a far more rich and interesting companion and partner.

Through this journey, I have come to see that the particular archetype to whom my heart resonated, Dionysos and his relationship in mythology to the feminine, is actually quite a bit larger than my personal pilgrimage of *Individuation*. I have discovered that his mysteries were celebrated in ancient and classical times as a liberating wholeness rite for Greek and Roman women. Thus, my story is supported by evidence of his particularly potent meaning for many women. As I delved deeper, a realization dawned that in fact the world we have created, and the maladies of alienation and real threat of annihilation, indeed have much to do with loss of the true Dionysian and his partnership with the feminine, in both her human and divine aspects.

Dionysos and the Healing of our World

We have been traveling a road of gradual estrangement from Source, both cosmic and from the earth—our natural environment, our home and our sustainer. We have created false authorities that find their justification in stories which promote fear and separation from our environment, from one another, and from ourselves. The battle of tribe against tribe, man against man, man against woman, and humankind's arrogant domination of the environment rather than collaboration has resulted in untold destruction. All have suffered: species, relationships, families, and humankind alienated from its own soul and from spirit.

Nations conquer other nations and manipulate core mythologies to substantiate their authority. These manipulations are evident in the exoteric teachings of religions that focus on the weakness of mankind. Their adherents are discouraged from finding individual connection to an inner authority and personal knowledge and intimacy with the subtler realms of being, both immediate and with the Macrocosm. These mandates are themselves a sin, in that the vision for a truly actualized, divinized humanity is rendered simply out of the question.[2] This divinized humanity is in fact our spiritual mandate; and we accomplish it by a simultaneous reverence for ourselves, one another, the earth, and the cosmos.

Our stories and our beliefs determine how we navigate our journey in life. The vast majority of people throughout history have been subjugated by stories and beliefs manipulated for economic and political advantage. The result is privilege and authority accorded to the few by religious and governmental control. Our sense of separateness from the earth, each other, and our own core essence fuels the economy but tears us apart internally and has destroyed much of our environment. The current state of world affairs is clear evidence of the ineffectiveness of the stories we have been accepting for far too long.

Our own souls cry out in distress through painful symptoms that are emotional, mental, and physiological. The objectification of our environment, of one another, and of ourselves has created a world in which it is easy to kill on every level—our relationships, our environment, and ourselves. And it is not a sacred killing that honors life in death but, worse, a living death, if not downright murder or suicide that finds a final expression in annihilation of soul and planet. A seemingly small but potent example is highlighted by the current crisis with the bees. Jungian analyst Frith Luton writes of the meaning of a tiny life-being who impacts our very existence on this planet:

> The symbolism of the bee... is vast... linking heaven and earth, god and man, the plant and animal kingdoms, sky gods and earth goddesses—including the supreme sun gods and the Great Mother Goddess.[3]

---

[2] The word for "sin" in both Hebrew and Greek translates as "to miss the mark," an archery term.

[3] Frith Luton, *Bees, Honey and the Hive*, p. 9.

The bees, with their profound symbolism, are fundamental to the availability of food for life on earth. Now even the bees are dying. The prevailing theory is that we are in some way polluting our environment and/or mishandling the bees, which is directly impacting the generation of crops. The cause may not be simple. It may be the result of our failure to understand the ecosystem as a kind of organism in itself. That failure has resulted in systemic effects, which are difficult to predict. The bees' pollination results in our crop production. This is but one example illustrating the imbalance in our relationship with nature, which is taking place on many levels. It is clear that the prevailing stories of how we view and interact with nature and with one another **must** change.

A Destructive Heritage of Biblical Story and Interpretation

The prevailing story in the Western world and anywhere influenced by Judeo-Christianity is the common understanding of Biblical Genesis. For more than two millennia, the West has been overshadowed by superficial interpretations of the story, leading to the conclusion of the culpability and inferiority of half of the human race, i.e., women. In this reading, it is woman's weakness that led to the "Fall," resulting in the struggles and hardship of all humankind. Earlier in history, evidence indicates that the feminine (woman—*Mater*, matter, and our Earth Mother) was highly venerated as the Life Giver, that is, She from whom Life sprung. That function was considered deeply sacred and miraculous. In fact, it is speculated that perhaps the male role in reproduction may have been unrecognized for quite some time. When it *was* recognized, it was seen as the activating force *in cooperation* with the feminine. And so it was the Earth, the mother of life, that was made fecund by the creative male energy. This produced new and renewing livingness.

Ultimately, one can say that both women and men are necessary for the miracle of life and should be equally valued. In her Kurgan

Hypothesis, archaeologist Marija Gimbutas argues that patriarchal nomads, who lived solely by hunting and had no experience of the growing cycle of the earth, were to blame for the demotion of the feminine.[4] Leonard Shlain, M.D. believes that literacy caused a shift from right- to left-brain dominance, and values, too, shifted as a result.[5] Whatever the causes and interpretation of stories, this distortion finds us at a crucial cultural crossroads with worldwide impact.

Misuse of Women and the Earth

What is happening to the earth is only different in scale to what is happening to women. A horrible and true illustration is the recently reported use of eight-year-old girls in Africa as suicide bombers. These girls are abducted, raped, and abused repeatedly, and then released only to be rejected by their own families on their return, thus making them perfect tools for an insane patriarchal death plan by their abductors. We are literally living in an insane world. The symptoms of underlying psychic pain and disorientation and the resulting horror must be addressed. Whatever is pure, lush, beautiful, green, and growing is at risk of being turned into a pit of spoilage and ruin from greed and fear—like these young girls—stolen, raped, and forced into death-dealing, or more mildly, prostitution. This is only one of countless examples. We might also include the "medication" of children who don't fit the established mold of educational norms and the rampant prescription of antidepressants and stimulants simply to function.

Redemption

Hints whisper through ancient mythologies that predate our deep descent into materialism. There have been currents flowing

---

[4] Marija Gimbutas, *The Prehistory of Eastern Europe, Part 1.*

[5] Leonard Shlain, *The Alphabet Versus the Goddess; The Conflict Between Word and Image.*

beneath the surface of history that offer hope and redemption from the chaos. Carl Jung and Joseph Campbell studied the stories of cultures throughout history and noted recurrent embodiments ("archetypes") of key aspects of the psyche, both instinctual and transpersonal. These figures are personifications of very real forces with which the conscious mind of humanity needs to contend. When in positive relationship, life continues harmoniously. When humanity ignores or exalts itself through hubris, negative consequences follow. A significant figure is the Greek god Dionysos. As we shall see, he finds analogous expression in the Hindu god Shiva, and in Egypt's Osiris. He represents the vital, powerfully phallic masculine spark that loves and is loved by the feminine. He is always imagined *in partnership* with her and never as her subjugator. And he has been demonized and repressed.

Dionysos is a masculine energy that calls us back to life and vitality. There is a crucial need to reclaim this vision and experience of the masculine. His repression has led to a twisted expression of all that he governs. Joy, sexuality, and transcendence become hedonism, pornography, and addiction. All archetypes have their shadow and the eruption of the shadow is inevitable with repression. Savagery, the dark side of Dionysos, finds expression in the unspeakable atrocities that we read or hear of every day in the news. The virtue of surrender becomes unconscious insanity, rather than regeneration and redemption. The dark side of Dionysos, in conjunction with the shadow of the more favored Western archetype, the solar Apollonic, creates a catastrophic cocktail of terrorism and "mass destruction" and, more immediately, destruction of one person at a time—at least psychically.

This book will establish a need for the positive gifts of Dionysos in the individual psyches of both men and women and in our collective partnership with the earth. I have given special attention to the historic and real role that Dionysos plays in women's *Individuation* and wholeness. The *Hieros Gamos* or *Sacred Marriage* was enacted in ancient times between women and this god, resulting in the continuance of life-giving sustenance, and more esoterically, in the completion of woman herself psychologically. Jungian Analytical Psychology explores the idea of *sacred marriage* as an inward event that matures a person, male and female. For a woman, finding a supportive *inner* masculine completes and empowers her. Her relationships are based on choice rather than neediness.

As women begin to reclaim their power and identity, a vital and non-patriarchal vision of the masculine and the *animus* is required. Dionysos was and is an ideal example of this masculine potency in right relationship with the feminine. What this study hopes to demonstrate is a vision of Dionysos as the *relational,* non-patriarchal expression of *Animus*—an *Erotic* (*Eros* indicating the "relating" factor) *Animus,* for women. *Sacred Marriage* serves as a contemporary initiation for women to wholeness and empowerment in the twenty-first century. Men, likewise, profoundly benefit personally and in relationship, by embracing Dionysian earth-centered, feminine-supporting, and passionate masculinity. Our world, too, might heal with a reclaiming and Integration of these essential and potent living images.

It is said that a god never dies, i.e., an archetype never dies. It is time to reclaim the virtues of Dionysos and bring them into positive relationship with the Apollonian progress (and there *has* been progress in terms of the clarity of thinking that Apollo represents) we have reached. What a remarkably vibrant archetype Dionysos still offers to the West! Here is a force and power so strong that it brings to the psyche a visceral and mystical sense of oneness with all of life, with life in the body, on the earth, and shared with all creatures. Rather than the materialistic view of objectifying nature as well as each other, isn't it time to bring a due respect and reverence to nature and ask not *what* is before us, but *who,* in all of our encounters? Isn't it time to grow out of a childish view of the sacred, which has resulted in the abuses of patriarchy and before that, matriarchy, and instead to evolve a more mature, responsible, and mutually cooperative *conscious* masculine and feminine perspective?

With great darkness, there is also great light. As we emerge from a polarity-focused and objectifying consciousness to one based more on relationships and systems, I notice a sparkling glimmer of hope that we may find once more a brotherhood and sisterhood with one another and with the amazing environment that is our earth home. We are children of the sun and, more grandly, of the cosmos.

How We Met

Dionysos…deep amethyst, crimson and wine-dark red, emerald and lapis…lavish velvets and brocades, the rich fur of a wildcat and the delicate warmth of the flower's petal…He is the sap that bleeds from the tree and the golden viscosity of the gift of the mother bees— honey. He is the ecstatic joy of hearts and bodies entangled and the "stop dead in your tracks" awe at the sudden clap of nature's power in thunder and earthquake. He is the drumbeat and the heart's rhythm. He is life's juice and the fire of spirit. From earliest memory, I have been his devotee.

I first met him in church. The pre-Vatican II Catholic Church of the early 1960s was still rich in imagery and mystical sensory delights. Jeweled stained glass, tender Italian statues of the Virgin and her Son with his fiery Sacred Heart, and attendant saints stood in quiet solemnity, gently lit by rows and rows of flickering ruby and indigo lights in the hushed darkness. At High Mass, the space was transformed into brilliance with exuberant light and sound. Gregorian chants inspired prayerful devotion. Frankincense and myrrh wafted in clouds of exotic perfume. The intermittent tinkling of three bells at special moments in the Mass punctuated the liturgy, elevating the soul in pure transcendence. These are the snippets of memory and deep soul imprint of childhood. The Sacred!

The drama of ritual and religious lushness imbued my world with mystery and magic. Alongside this sumptuous banquet, the neutered grey of Cold War images glared on the television screen. Backyard concrete bomb shelters were a thriving business; and the shrill call of the Friday drill siren called us children to fall to the floor and fold fetal-like beneath our desks (quite absurdly, in retrospect) so we would know just what to do should there be a nuclear attack. This was the world of an American Catholic school child in that strange era.

At Saint Charles Borromeo School, I fell in awe and in love with my kindergarten teacher, Sister Mary St. Suzanne. She was a vision of beauty and dignity as she swept into our classroom dressed in the traditional religious "habit." She was young and pretty and I now realize she must have been in her mid-twenties. Most importantly, she was *HOLY*! I decided there and then that this was what I wanted to be when I grew up, a "Sister," that is, a *Holy Woman* dedicated to the Divine.

The first significant step was preparation for the sacrament of Holy Communion in the second grade. We had a hefty catechism and prayers to memorize, and we learned to thoroughly examine our hearts and minds at the tender age of seven in preparation for the grand initiation. The Sacrament of Confession would prepare us to meet Him, in the Sacrament to follow, Holy Communion. We, as little girls, wore the equivalent of a bouffant white wedding dress to meet and commune with Him for the first time under the auspices of the Host, the visible presence of Christ. The "Jesus" we courted, in utmost purity, was a tender and loving first *animus* for the barely unfurled bud of the little-girl feminine.

For the remaining years of childhood, my favorite game was playing "Sister" or performing the Mass (somehow being a girl didn't inhibit my priestly fantasy). The *Lives of the Saints*—the "how to" books of saintliness—were preferred reading. The gift of my first teacher was a lifelong love affair with the Spirit and with the *mysteries*. That young nun accompanied my very first steps into the hall of knowledge and the temple of reverence, beauty, and wisdom represented by the Dionysian mysteries as I now understand them.

Fast forward. At sixteen, I fell in love with a boy. He was Venezuelan, of Spanish and Basque descent, and had the dark elongated, ethereal presence of an El Greco painting. Here was my Dionysos in the flesh! This was my first love, and it lasted three alternately ecstatic and agonizing years. For several days, or weeks, or months, there would be bliss; then his inexplicable coldness and withdrawal. The pain reached outer limits with a culmination of high school drama and pathos. I came as close as I ever have to the possibility of suicide. I survived by burying the grief and walking into a new life, finding romance and marriage as quickly as possible to obliterate the memory. If I could counsel my younger self, I would advise her to experience whatever is in her heart fully, to mourn and allow the heart its process. I would suggest she not rush to a cure without a healing. In time, I did, of course, heal, in spite of the detours and defenses and all the further messes we make trying to avoid one.

This is the story of what love inaugurated. First love was only, and yet significantly, the beginning of a lifelong process of *Individuation*. Many years later, upon reading the myth of Ariadne and Dionysos, I recognized my youthful experience in the plight of Ariadne, abandoned by her lover on the shore of Naxos. The Venezuelan had been my Theseus masquerading as, and in fact anticipating, the true Dionysos of my soul. I had projected a god onto a very human boy, clearly a weight too heavy for anyone, especially an adolescent boy, to carry. But passions run strong and wild in the awakening romantic heart.

The happy ending of Ariadne's story is that the god Dionysos comes for her. She becomes his bride and an immortal. My understanding of this is that Ariadne finds a vibrant and faithful *animus* who supports her femininity and redeems her bruised and bereft psyche within her interior Self. Gods are not human men, after all. This *animus* is *not* another better man, but the development of her own soul into an unforeseen wholeness. Life does not always offer up "happy endings" in the outer world; but a real sense of inner wholeness is possible for the woman who looks deeply into her experiences, retrieving the gifts of life's challenges. In recognizing the sacred partner within her own soul, her personality becomes a vessel for the larger, truer Self seeking to live through her.

Now, a half-century after that first human love and others, I find myself living in the land of Dionysos—the wine country of Napa, California—and marvel at fate and destiny. I had no intention to move here. Life's circumstances lined up in synchronistic fashion to bring me to a precious retreat overlooking the bounty of Dionysos, the vineyards. From this holy place, I sing of his joyousness and power and hope to inform and inspire his honor.

This study is divided into three parts. Each serves a distinct purpose.

Part One provides a historical and mythic foundation. It reviews the origins of the archetype of Dionysos, the myths and the mysteries associated with him in the ancient world.

Part Two explores the continuing significance and psychological value of Dionysos, the story of his marriage to Ariadne, to Feminine Individuation, and the needs of men in relationship to the Masculine within.

Part Three looks at the societal—especially in terms of the struggle for freedom—and personal expressions of the values represented by Dionysos and Ariadne that figure today. The connection between respect for women, nature, and the manifold expressions of gender are related to this extraordinarily invigorating and healing archetypal pattern.

Part One

ORIGINS, MYTHS & MYSTERIES

1

WHO IS DIONYSOS?
WHY DOES HE MATTER?

More than an entity, Dionysos is a full sensory field. When writing about my experience as a Catholic child with Dionysos, I am describing the Dionysian ambience of the Catholic Christ and the Church of my youth.

The Greek gods and goddesses can be likened to the colors of *soul;* and this was my soulful experience of Christianity in the early 1960s, and later in visiting European churches, which continue to be drenched energetically in two thousand years (or more, in the case of sites built on ancient temples) of devotion.

Dionysos is *not* Christ, but there *is* a resonance. Christ emanates from the world of *Spirit*, from the original "White Light" that refracts through the *soul* prism into the multicolored spectrum. Christ's colors and signs are the colors and signs of Dionysos. But Dionysos is of the *soul* world, not *spirit*, though he points toward that higher realm. As a *soul* frequency, he is not necessarily moral and partakes of the many vicissitudes—the peaks and valleys—of soul experience. Christ, on the other hand, is a higher frequency. While Dionysos punishes severely those who disdain him, Christ teaches the higher value of compassion. Christ is about Love and Life. Dionysos is about Passion and Life. Though resonating at different frequencies, the two are related.

Christ is traditionally depicted with a cloak of red—the quintessential color associated with life force.

He began and ended His ministry with the miracle of wine. The grapevine is their shared quintessential symbol. Like Dionysos and the Great Mother, Christ and the Madonna are not at odds, but positively related. Christ and Dionysos are both accompanied and loved by women to whom they show great care and respect. Both are liberators and both are egalitarian—free of elitism, xenophobia, and all other phobias in fact.

While this is not a book on religion, it *is* a treatise on the values and virtues of a particular soul potency and competency. Those values include a presence to—and respect for—life, reverence towards the earth and one another, and the dance of partnership between the masculine and feminine and humanity and earth, and the cultivation of connection and joy.

It is important to highlight what Dionysos is **not**. He is not hedonism, irresponsibility, nor pure license. These aspects that have been associated with him are actually the result of the abuse and perversion of the Dionysian virtues. The aim of Dionysos is not debauchery but a loosening of ego to allow soul expression and to invite the experience of indwelling Spirit. When debauchery ensued in his name, his rites had devolved into a corrupted facsimile. H. Jeremiah Lewis, a present-day devotee of Dionysos, writes:

> Dionysos has nothing to do with addiction. Addiction is bondage, and Dionysos is all about freedom. Indulgence taken too far is slavery. And so Dionysos is there to help those who are battling against the invisible chains that keep them from living an authentic and self-governed life. Dionysos is the one who invented the custom of watering down wine, and who taught the ancients to drink temperately... Dionysos can help us pare down these things [addictive behaviors], open us to a more expansive vision of life...Dionysian asceticism

isn't about denying our pleasures or the world—it's about reshaping them, intensifying them, redirecting them into other avenues…the path of discipline and denial can be a powerful tool towards that end.[6]

How wonderful and perfect that in our frailty we might call on the god to help heal our tendency towards overindulgence! Lewis points out that Dionysos is about being *all* that we can be, the best that we can be, the most present and vital. Blaming him for the perversion of his service is dishonor and disrespect.

Dionysos, the God

In Greek mythology, Dionysos is described as the first and last of the gods, the thirteenth god of the Olympian pantheon.[7] Just as the Sun burns brightly in the midst of twelve zodiacal formations, and Jesus was the thirteenth in a circle of twelve apostles, he is the special "thirteenth." He has a strong connection with Apollo, the sun god, whom we will explore in the chapter dedicated to his worship in ancient Greece. While Apollo is associated with the daytime sun, Dionysos was seen as the sun in the darkness—an Underworld, interior sun—the radiant black sun. Dionysos is a tantric god associated with the Hindu Shiva by the scholar Alain Daniélou, bringing together the opposites in ecstatic and transcendent union.[8]

He is known as the god of life, of death and rebirth. He is the "fireborn," the "moist" god, the "phallic god" as well as "the womanly

---

[6] H. J. Lewis, *Ecstatic*, p. 13.

[7] David Leeming, *Oxford Companion of World Mythology,* p. 165.

[8] My use of the word *tantra* refers to the Tibetan (Vajrayana) understanding of the term, which is based on the belief that everything is permeated by a single power (Shakti), which manifests in three ways: feminine, masculine, and the union of the two. It is that union which is a goal of tantric practice.

one."[9] He is the god of divine ecstasy and, when his mysteries are abused, of excess in drunkenness and even madness. As the god of wine, he put mortals in touch with the Divine:

> …people felt about Dionysus as about no other god. He was not only outside of them, he was within them too. They could be transformed by him into being like him. The momentary sense of exultant power wine drinking could give was only a sign to show men that they had within them more than they knew; they could themselves be divine.[10]

At home in the forests and mountains, as well as the sea, he has no love for the cities and the social conventions of urban living. His rites are most often performed at night. This god is surrounded and loved by women. A vegetation god (the unruly vine and ivy, sacred to him, whisper his presence), he is also a god associated with animals. His totemic powers include the bull, the goat, the panther, leopard, tiger, fawn, ass, snake, and dolphin. These animal totems are obviously varied but meaningfully so. They include the oppositions of ferocity and gentleness… of the fiery, earthy, and watery elements of nature. He is as wild and untamed as nature herself. The Greeks had two words for "life": *Bio* and *Zoë*. Whereas *Bio* refers to "the characteristic traits of a specified life, the outlines that distinguish one living thing from another. *Zoë*, on the other hand, represents the livingness of all life. *Zoë* is the life pulse that reverberates through all of creation. Dionysos *is* *Zoë*.

In Crete, Dionysos appears as the lord of the wild beasts, consort of the Great Goddess. In Carl Kerényi's words, he is the "Image

---

[9] Walter Friedrich Otto, *Dionysus,* p. 176.

[10] Edith Hamilton, *Mythology,* p. 60.

of the Indestructible Life.[11]" Heraclitus tells us that Dionysos, representing the vibrancy of the life force itself, is also Hades, the god of death.[12] This is a remarkable observation. This god, in fact, straddles two extremes in a tension so taut that it borders the polarities of life and death and threatens the hinterlands in between.

In astrology, one of the twelve houses on the zodiacal wheel resembles his profound energy. The eighth house rules "sex, death and transformation." Interesting bedfellows, seemingly opposite, they are yet so deeply resonant. The concerns of this "house" reveal an archetypal affinity. Dionysos, too, brings us to the gates of life and death and the possibility of alchemical transformation in passing betwixt and between those tremendous forces.

Scholars have recognized Dionysos as carrying the same symbolic energy of all dying and resurrecting gods, including Osiris of Egypt, the Persian Tammuz, and, of course, Christ. Plutarch, who officiated as priest at the Temple of Delphi, said Dionysos and Osiris are one. Though Dionysos is thought to have been the final addition to the Greek pantheon, this god is also one of the oldest conceptions of the divine masculine. And he is a god who is helpmate and consort of the fertile feminine, never her adversary or her master.

> In Dionysus, borders *join* that which we usually believe
> to be separated by borders. The philosopher is also a
> lover; Socrates is a drinking Silenus; the riotous
> Dionysos has but one wife, Ariadne. Dionysus presents
> us with borderline phenomena, so that we cannot tell
> whether he is mad or sane, wild or sober, sexual or
> psychic, male or female, conscious or unconscious.
> Kerényi says that, wherever Dionysos appears, the
> "border" is also manifested. He rules the borderlands of

---

[11] Carl Kerényi, *Dionysos*, p. xxxii.

[12] Guthrie, *Orpheus and Greek Religion*, Herakleitos, p. 226.

our psychic geography. There the Dionysian dance takes place; neither this nor that, an ambivalence—which also suggests that wherever ambivalence appears, there is a possibility for Dionysian consciousness.[13]

He is a liminal god, who transcends containment, confinement, and static definition. He represents the ancient, matrifocal ways that long preceded the coming of the "sky fathers" of the Indo-European tribes. He is a nature deity and the force of nature itself. Dionysos, first and foremost, as an earth-centered god, is "dark." This darkness, long associated with evil by Western white culture, is an ally of the rich fecund earth, of the "She" who gives birth to all life in her secret recesses.

His domain, is in Plutarch's words...not only the liquid fire in the grape but the sap thrusting in a young tree, the blood pounding in the veins of the young animal, all the mysterious and uncontrollable tides that ebb and flow in the life of nature[14]...He is the principle of animal life...the hunted and the hunter—the un-restrained potency...His cult was originally an attempt on the part of human beings to achieve communion with his potency. The psychological effect was to liberate the instinctive life in man from the bondage imposed on it by reason and social custom: the worshipper became conscious of a strange new vitality, which he attributed to the god's presence within him...he is not only with the Master of Life but with his fellow worshippers; and is one also with life on earth.[15]

---

[13] James Hillman, *The Myth of Analysis*, p. 275.

[14] E.R. Dodds, Introduction to *The Bacchae*, p. xii.

[15] Dodds, Introduction to *The Bacchae*, p. xx.

Dionysos has been called the god of ecstasy, madness, of the dance, of theater, of the mask, of mead and wine, and all expressions of the transcendent experience.

> To affirm the Dionysian is to recognize and appreciate the place of pain and death in life, and to tolerate the full range from death to life and from pain to ecstasy, including wounding, in which one is "delivered" from the flat ennui of numbing conformity to cultural and familial expectations.[16]

When defamed, he caused madness, and yet he also liberated his devotees from madness, certainly from the madness of mechanical, spiritless life and from the alienation that plagues the rational mind.

What Happened?

For many thousands of years, the qualities of this deity were honored, feared, and loved. His presence inspired awe and respect. So how was his awesome presence and power demoted to the laughable god of hedonism or, worse, the embodiment of evil?

Alain Daniélou distinguishes two distinct sources of religion, the natural and the urban.[17] Nature religions experience the holy in the vibrant and dynamic creative forces streaming from the Sun and the Earth and her elements. The world of spirit and matter are seen as inextricably linked. Everything is alive. It is an experiential, animistic, ecstatic, and mystical worldview. This is the religious expression to which Dionysos belonged.

With the Mycenaean period in Greece, which lasted from 1600-1100 BC, a second form of religion evolved, which was tied to the world of communal city life. Belief structures and priestly hierarchy took

---

[16] James Hillman, *The Puer Papers*, p. 176

[17] Alain Daniélou, *Shiva and Dionysos*, p. 13

precedence over personal revelation. From the city's point of view, the ecstatic, untamed, irrational edging sometimes on the tooth and claw of nature was viewed with suspicion as threatening social order. Sometimes downright persecution ensued. In the Greek Classical period's stories of the fates of King Pentheus, as described in Euripides' play *The Bacchae;* the daughters of the Thracian King Lycurgus; as well as those of Kings Proteus and Minyas, all of whom were afflicted with madness for having refused to receive the rites of Dionysos, demonstrate the tension and, at times, the conflict between the rational and natural worlds.

> Psychologically, the story of his (Dionysos') loss is the triumph of rationality over irrationality; thinking over feeling; the concrete "masculine" ideals of power, aggression, and progress over the intangible "feminine" values of receptivity, growth and nurturing. As the patriarchal religions gained in power, the old matrifocal ways of Dionysos were diminished and finally lost.[18]

The defeat of Dionysos and the matrifocal values spelled the beginning of a growing culture of irreverence and objectification on every front. It is not too great a stretch to thread that loss to today's threat of human and planetary annihilation.

On the Greek mainland in Delphi, the god of reason, Apollo, was worshipped at the same temple as Dionysos. These deities and their values were seen as two complementary and symbiotic halves, embodying a balance in the relationship of humankind to nature and to one another. With the rise of urban and rational values, sadly, Apollo supplanted him.

> Apollo gradually came to represent analytical thought and the preservation of law and order. The unpre-

---

[18] Robert Johnson, *Ecstasy*, p. 15.

dictable, irrational, ecstatic Dionysus had no place in this scheme—was in fact, the enemy of it. The chief god was now officially to be found "up there" in the sky as the sun, Apollo. "Down here," the earth, the realm of Dionysus, was shorn of its power…Dionysus fared no better with Jews or the Christians, who turned his goat image into the very face of the devil.[19]

Eventually, reason, analysis, and hierarchical values, rather than liminal states of consciousness, fluidity, and mutually dependent systems, became guiding virtues. A linear historical perspective replaced the cyclic and synthetic orientation of agriculturally-based societies. In a mythic-religious sense, the sky gods subjugated the Earth Mother; in the process, her consort/son was demonized.

With the coming of Christianity, Dionysos along with the nature god, Pan, with whom he shared the totem of the goat, came to serve as the incarnation of evil, the devil. The strength and power of the goddess was largely eclipsed by the Church's emphasis on the quiet humility of the Mother of God. Women, in general, became a suspicious presence whose best place was in the roles of tamed wife, mother or nun, always second to male authority.

Reclaiming the qualities and sensibilities of the Dionysian is to bring back a soulful, enlivened balance between the sexes and between humankind and nature. Our Earth herself, I believe, longs for communion with her children. A return to the gifts of Dionysos might bring healing to her and to both men and women.

But I jump ahead. Let us travel back, back in time to when Dionysos was known far and wide and honored as the vitality of life itself, as the last and youngest of the gods and the first and oldest, and seek the origin of his worship.

---

[19] Johnson, *Ecstasy*, p. 16.

THRACE

BITHYNIA

Chrysopolis

Byzantium

PROPONTIS

PHRYGIA

Aegospotami

Hellespont

LYDIA

Sardis

MACEDON

Amphipolis

CHALCIDICE

Potidaea

Scione

Thasos

Samothrace

Lesbos

Mytilene

Arginusae

Chios

Notium

Ephesus

Samos

Miletus

CARIA

Hallicarnassus

Rhodes

THESSALY

EPIRUS

Epidamnus

Corcyra

Delphi

Scyros

Euboea

Chalcis

Eretria

Delion

Thebes

BOEOTIA

Megara

Athens

Aegina

Sicyon

Corinth

Mycenae

Argos

Mantinea

Elis

Olympia

PELOPONNESE

Sparta

LACONIA

MESSENIA

Pylos

Corinthian Gulf

Zacynthus

AEGEAN SEA

IONIA

Delos

Naxos

Paros

Melos

0   100 miles

0   170 kilometers

2

ROOTS

From nowhere and everywhere, he is brand new and has always been. He is palpable and yet elusive. What are his roots? Where did he come from?

Dionysos is said to have come from Thebes in Boeotia (mainland Greece), from Phrygia (now part of Turkey) and Lydia (in Western Asia Minor), from Crete, and even from Libya and India. The Greek historian and geographer Pausanisas (1st century A.D.) tells us Dionysos came from Thrace (an area consisting of present-day southeastern Bulgaria, northeastern Greece and Western Turkey)[20], while French historian and Shaivite Hindu scholar Alain Daniélou, makes a compelling argument that the Hindu Shiva and Western Dionysos are in fact essentially one, implying that Dionysian religion may actually be Indian in origin, as it predates the Greek form.

India

Alain Daniélou looks to the Shiva cult of the Dravidians, the pre-Indo-Aryan people who lived on the Indian subcontinent, as the source of the Dionysian archetype. He dates evidence of Shiva worship as far back as 10,000-8,000 B.C. With the invasion and domination by Aryan tribes, the cult was integrated into the Vedic religion of the conquerors.

---

[20] Carl Kerényi, *Dionysos,* p. 137.

Like Dionysos, Shiva is described as a bull god, infant god, god abandoned by his mother, god of double birth, dying god, god of the vine as well as numerous forms of vegetation, a horned one, bearded god, and adolescent god.[21] Dionysos and Shiva share many of the same totems, symbols and celebration, including a close association with and veneration of the divine feminine.

> Shaivism was codified during the sixth millennium B.C. Starting from this period, Shivaite rites and symbols began to appear both in India and in Europe: the cult of the bull, the phallos, the ram, the snake, the Lady of the Mountains, as well as ecstatic dances, the swastika, the labyrinth, sacrifices etc...The megalithic monuments and symbolic representations testifying to its presence are so widespread: the traditions, legends, rites and festivities deriving from it are found in so many regions, that it appears everywhere as one of the main sources of later religion...However, only in India have these traditions and what are known as Dionysiac rites been maintained without interruption from prehistoric times until today. Greek texts speak of Dionysus' mission to India, and Indian texts of the expansion of Shaivism towards the West.[22]

The essential mythic pattern here—of nature experienced as Mother and her Son/Lover who is born, dies and rises again, is repeated throughout ancient civilizations. It finds expression in Shiva and Shakti of India, the Sumerian Inanna and Dumuzi, Ishtar and Tammuz of Mesopotamia, in Isis and Osiris/ Horus of Egypt, and in Dionysos and the Great Mother, Rhea, as well as his consort bride, Ariadne.

---

[21] Alain Daniélou, *Shiva and Dionysus*, pp. 50-51.

[22] Daniélou, *Shiva and Dionysus*, p. 32.

Egypt

In *Dionysos, Archetypal Image of the Indestructible Life*, Carl Kerényi makes a fascinating argument for the connection between the cult of Dionysos and Egyptian religion and practice. The Egyptian New Year was celebrated at the heliacal rising of the star Sirius in our calendar month of July. Annually, in late spring, Sirius descends below the horizon and is not visible for seventy days. When the star appears again, a remarkable blessing would come to the Egyptians each year, the flooding of the Nile. The flood allowed planting and cultivation, which would have been impossible in the Saharan climate without the waters of the Nile. Sirius was the inspiration for Egypt's first calendar and that calendar was sacred as well as secular.

As nature and religion were seamlessly integrated in the ancient world, physical and spiritual renewal were celebrated during this high point in summer. The goddesses Hathor and Isis were associated with Sirius. Isis' husband, Osiris, was identified with nearby Orion. Sirius is, in fact, a double star, and the mythology of the Dogon tribe near Egypt associates Sirius A with Isis, and the smaller, heavier Sirius B with Osiris. Possibly, the Egyptians, too, made this association. The gods and great teachers of mankind were believed to have come from Sirius, and the worthy souls of the dead returned there.

The cosmic event of Sirius, the second brightest star in the sky (the Sun's being the first brightest), disappearing for seventy days and then reappearing, was considered a *second* birth of the light with the same significance as the winter solstice, but with more cosmic connotations. As we shall see in the Orphic Dionysian mysteries, Dionysos, like Osiris, experienced death and rebirth and that rebirth was interpreted as more than simply a renewal of nature. It was seen as an event of *spiritual* significance.[23] Thus, what occurred to the star Sirius (its disappearance and return) was seen as a cosmic representation of the spiritual death and rebirth possible for mankind and illustrated in the myths of both Osiris and Dionysos. Sirius, then, is the stellar expression of Osiris and Dionysos, the prototype of death (to humanity's limited consciousness) and spiritual rebirth.

The name for Sirius in Egypt was *Sothis*. 'Sirius' is originally a Greek word, *Seiros,* meaning *sparkling* or *scorching.* In fact, what we call the "Dog Days" of summer, known for their extreme heat, originated from the days especially sacred to the Dog Star, Sirius. "Bright" and "hot" were themes very much associated with Sirius, as well as the flow of water and the liquid in nature (as evidenced by the flooding of the Nile), the same essential and opposing but complementary themes we find associated with Dionysos.

Kerényi notes that the major religious and political sites of Crete and Greece marked their New Year on the day of the heliacal rising of Sirius, just as the Egyptians did. He surmises that this custom must have come from Egypt to mainland Greece through the Minoan civilization on Crete. No agricultural imperative, as existed in Egypt, accounted for the timing on Crete or in Greece for this celebration.

The Egyptian Cretan Connection and the Star Sirius

In Crete, mead (honey wine), predating the cultivation of grapes for wine, was traditionally brewed precisely at this same time and was part of a highly sacred festival. Its fermentation process was scheduled to conclude on *the first day of the year of Sirius.*[24] Roman scholar Pliny associated Sirius with the origin of honey at the time of

---

[23] Albert Pike, *Morals and Dogma of the Ancient and Accepted Scottish Rite of Freemasonry,* p. 586.

[24] Kerényi, *Dionysos,* p. 38.

its rising.[25] Here, we see a direct connection between Sirius, honey, and the first spirited drink associated with Dionysos.

The hive, itself, was seen as *the* tangible expression of *Zoë*, the overwhelming life force, while the production of honey was not only the pure expression of the sweetness of life's essence but also was, and remains, an essential process in the preservation of the life cycle.

> Bees are nature's great pollinators, so they play a crucial role in the biological web of life. They also have a central role as culture bringers and psychopomps in the creation myths of many lands and folk stories concerned with regeneration and *zoë*...Bees...and flowers are closely linked...flowers are essential as sources of nectar and pollen...It is the often-golden centres of flowers that attract the bees. In return, bees are essential for fertilizing plants—pollinating flowers, cross-pollinating fruit trees and doing much to ensure the setting of the fruit. This world of flowering and fruiting (a particular kind of regeneration) is also central in alchemical symbolism...[26]

The bees (the Queen, her chosen drone and the worker bees), the hive, and the production of the miraculous nectar were seen as numinous and overwhelmingly holy. By analogy, the Queen Bee could have easily represented the Great Mother and her chosen drone, the god/lover who dies in order to renew the life of the hive through their union. Artifacts survive from ancient Crete depicting the bee in a goddess shape.

The hive itself, with its hexagonal structure, is a geometric configuration which occurs with the union of opposites (it is formed

---

[25] Richard Hinckley Allen, *Star Names: Their Lore and Meaning*, p. 129.

[26] Frith Luton, *Bees Honey and the Hive*, p. 14.

by the intersection of two opposing triangles that symbolically represent Heaven and Earth, Spirit and Matter, Male and Female), emblematic of the love union, and which engenders new life. Honey, and the pollen from which it is made, is almost universally regarded as the food of the gods. It is a preserver and it never putrefies. The fermentation of honey creates an elixir which, like grape wine, lifts and lightens consciousness. The honey wine (mead), like grape wine, is alchemical in that it requires human intervention to produce something "en-spirited."[27] Neither mead nor wine occur by themselves in nature. A collaboration between human and nature invites the in-spirit-ment by the god.

Kerényi, too, associates the fiery star Sirius, the fiery (hot) time of year, and the fire of life that *was* Dionysos to the Minoans and the Greeks. The glow of actual fires from caves associated with the sacred hive, with honey, and with initiation into the mysteries was reportedly seen on Crete and Greece at this time of year. Furthermore, Kerényi connects Dionysos with Sirius in noting the similarity of the words *Iachos* (a Cretan variation on the name Bacchus) and *Iakar,* the Minoan name for Sirius. Finally, the ancient Greeks themselves considered the vine itself to be a gift of the star Sirius.

In a tractate written by Plutarch and addressed to Klea, the head of the college of Thyiads (the Dionysian priestesses), it is mentioned that she was also a devotee of the "the holy rites of Osiris" and that they agree that Dionysos and Osiris are one, and both represent "*the liquid element.*"[28]

The basic properties of liquid include an ability to change shape by flowing; its elements and molecules are not in fixed positions. It conforms to the shape that contains it. Liquids have a definite volume and they are not compressible. Dionysos represents these qualities. He

---

[27] Alchemy, as we shall see later, was the art of refining what appears in nature and required the intervention of man to achieve.

[28] Martin P. Nilsson, *The Dionysiac Mysteries of the Hellenistic and Roman Age,* p. 38.

moves, he shifts, he changes. He spills out, but he cannot be forced into a smaller space than his nature warrants. Dionysos, in fact, is said to have invented honey.[29]

The Minoan Civilization

The Minoan civilization of ancient Crete (2000-1400 B.C.E.) saw the Western debut of the archetype in India, called Shiva and, in Egypt, Osiris. Carl Kerényi and Walter Otto, both scholars of Greek mythology, have argued for a strong, very ancient and *indigenous* Dionysian tradition. Far from being a late arrival in the pantheon of the gods, they point to the discovery of the name Dionysos found in Cretan Linear script dating from 1200 B.C. in Pylos, on the Greek Mainland.[30] On Crete, there are numerous iconographic parallels, including the bull, the snake, the horns, the he-goat, the phallic pillar, and the ecstatic dances of the Kouretes (the male dancers who venerated the Mother Goddess on Crete). The Minoan religion, like that of the Indian Dravidian peoples, was oriented towards nature.

In our search to understand Dionysos, it is important to appreciate the Minoan worldview that gave birth to him in the West. The Minoans were "synthetic" in their thinking; that is, they focused on the interrelatedness of experience, in contrast to the later development of the Aristotelian or analytic approach of distinguishing differences and separating elements as a way of knowledge. Dionysos as a nature god was, and is, indivisible from the relational fabric of nature.[31] Natural rhythm and movement characterized the Minoan style.

The Minoans created a civilization whose characteristics were the love of life and nature, and an art strongly

[29] Ovid, *Fasti III*, 736.
[30] Kerényi, *Dionysos*, p. 68, 69.
[31] Charles Herberger, *The Thread of Ariadne*, p. 26.

imbued with charm and elegance...Motion is its ruling characteristic; the figures move with lovely grace, the decorative designs whirl and turn...The secret life of nature is outspread...a hymn to Nature as Goddess seems to be heard from everywhere, a hymn of joy and grace.[32]

As we have seen, the religion of Crete, like all religions honoring nature, venerated the Great Mother. She is seen in frescoes and on seals as the "Lady of the Mountain," "Lady of the Snakes," the moon goddess, the Earth Mother, and the bee goddess. A male figure is also found, whom archaeologists have named "Lord of the Beasts," as well as the "Bull God"—an ubiquitous motif in Cretan art. He is "the seed" and he shares in the seed's potential as well as in its mortality.[33] He fructifies the vegetation cycle represented by the goddess. His epithet, Bromios (Bacchus), which means the "Thunderer" or "Roaring One," evokes the fiery nature of the potency and intensity of his life force. However, in keeping with the natural cycle, he also is a dying god. This theme of death and rebirth, seen over and over again in Greece, Egypt, as well as in the Middle East, is carried forward in the Cretan, and later Greek, Dionysos.

From Crete, we move on now to Greece, where more extensive records remain describing his festivals, and his profound value and meaning, in the yearly round of life, death and renewal.

---

[32] Kerényi, *Dionysos*, p. 6, quoting Nikolaos Platon's Introduction, *A Guide to the Archaeological Museum of Heraklion.*

[33] Herberger, *The Thread of Ariadne*, p. 26.

3

FLOWERING

Greece

It is in Greece that we find the flowering of Dionysian celebrations, rites, myth, and mysteries. It is here that we find his close association with wine and further illustrations of the significance of his rites, both for ensuring fertility and for balancing the psyche of what was becoming an increasingly more civilized and tame culture. We will begin our consideration of Dionysos and the power and color of his influence on Greek life with a brief look at his four most renowned and popular festivals—*Lesser Dionysia, the Anthesteria, The Greater Dionysia,* and the *Lenaia.* These celebrations followed the viticulture cycle of the year.

Joy, Sex, Comedy, and Tragedy

Let us imagine what it might have been like the evening of the festival celebrated near the winter solstice. Perhaps there was a young girl named Althea, who was one of the lucky females to have been taught by her mother to write. Let us imagine her thoughts that December night.

Alchemy of the Heart

Althea's Diary, Athens, Winter, 406 B.C.

Dear Diary,

It was very cool and crisp this morning. The sun did not rise until nearly 8:00…but the day was gloriously sunny after the dark and dreary days we have had for so many long days! We were all a little worried it might rain, as the clouds had been heavy. But a refreshing wind came in the night, maybe brought by the god himself! We had hardly slept a wink waiting for the festival that makes life bright, even when the days are short. It is the feast of the birth of the god of joy! The celebration brings us all together as a people. It is so much fun! And blessed be, from now on the sun will warm and brighten the earth a little bit longer.

The port became a carnival today! My best friends, Alexia, Delia and Chloe, spent the night so we could rise early and make it down to Piraeus for the festivities before all the good viewing sites were gone. We found my brothers, Nikias and Marcion, had joined in the games. They made such a funny spectacle, acting all proud…then working hard to stay atop the greased wineskin. Falling, of course! Everyone was sipping and toasting with the new wine. Even my little brother, Kyros, who is only six, had his first taste but only after we had made the proper pouring forth to the god.

The one-legged races were hilarious. And then there were the feasts—every sort of delicacy imaginable…and the lamb…yum! Oh, but I forgot to mention, the dancing and the singing in the streets and the procession with the grand emblem of Life itself, the phallos of the god, accompanied by girls carrying the baskets we normally use for threshing, and then sometimes the fruits of harvest, and then, too, for carrying infants. They are perfect for that purpose! All joy to new life! May the sun grow ever brighter! Spring will come again!

The Lesser Dionysia

What Althea is describing is a trip to one of what would have been considered the outer environs of Athens, and the ensuing festivities of the Rural or Lesser Dionysia, close to the winter solstice.

Having been conceived of Zeus by the mortal woman, Semele, in early March, Dionysos' birth was celebrated in December. Near the temple of *Dionysos Limnaeos* (Dionysos of the swamps), Athenians poured out wine libations to the god. New wine was drawn from the casks and brought to the festival to be drunk. The merriment included songs, dances, plays, and games, including the *Askoliosmos*, in which men attempted to balance on a well-greased wineskin, one-legged races, and feasts.[34] It included a jubilant procession in which an effigy of an enormous erect phallos was carried accompanied by women carrying *liknons*. The *liknon* was a long basket used to further separate the wheat from the chaff after threshing. It was also used to carry infants because of its ideal shape, as well as to bear first fruits. The symbolic resonance is clear.

* * *

Althea's Diary, the 12th day of Gemalion (mid-January), 405 B.C.

Dear Diary,
Today begins the festival of Lenaia. Father paid the 2 obols each for us to see the comedies. Tickets are precious now because the plays are so popular. I'm glad

---

[34] Kerényi, *Dionysos*, p. 324.

Father knows the people who can get us good seats. Father is very keen on the fact that Aristophanes' play, *The Frogs* will be performed. I don't know anything about it, but Father says from what he has heard, it absolutely says what our city has been going through and comments on what has happened to the great art of tragedy. Things haven't been right for awhile. The war has been hard on us. And did you know, Sophocles died just now? Father is quite upset by that news. I am hoping that he will feel better after the comedies, especially *The Frogs*.

Lenaia

Tragedies and comedies were performed at this winter festival, with the emphasis on comedies. The festival lasted three to four days, with one comedy being performed each day, and two days of tragedies. The lightening effect of comedies was a relief during the winter tedium. There was a procession, overseen by the Archon (Athenian King), which involved revellers who mocked and insulted everyone in good jest. It was a sort of worship through laughter. The *Lenaia* is thought to have been celebrated in the Agora (the marketplace) and the performances to have taken place in the Theatre of Dionysos on the Acropolis.

There may have also been an additional ritual for women as evinced by the name *Lenaia*. *Lenai* is another name for *Maenad*, referring to the *lenos*, the wine press. The Lenaian vessels illustrate women dancing, making music, carrying the *thyrsus*, and pouring out wine before a pillar with the mask of Dionysos.[35]

Let's take a look at what Althea might have written two months later:

---

[35] Kerenyi, *Dionysos*, p. 284.

Althea's Diary, March, 405 B.C.

Dear Diary,

It has been two moons since the carnival at Solstice, and one since Lenaia. How the world has changed! Tiny green shoots appeared overnight on the dark twisted vines. So sweet, like tiny green babes, all fresh and bright and new.

Today we begin our three-day festival, the sacred *Anthesteria,* which will ensure a good spring and our city's abundance. I can't believe it! I have been chosen as one of the girls to begin the festivities celebrating the wedding of our queen to the Holy One. Mother has made me a special snow-white tunic just for the occasion! Alexia and Chloe have been chosen too, but I feel so sad for Delia. She has to stay at home with her sick grandmother. We will miss her, but I will try to remember everything so I can tell her all about it as if she were with us as well.

So here is what we get to do. We will swing and swing and swing to try and best each other in reaching the heights. Meanwhile, the priestesses will be paying homage at the 14 shrines. And then there will be the grand procession leading our lovely queen to meet the god. All along there will be the celebrating: the drinking of wine of course, and feasting, and joking and joy. Even the slaves aren't slaves during this time, and the high and mighty better act like everyone else. No one dares to act superior, we are all the same before the god. He doesn't like it when people are left out or looked down upon. It's one big party. And we need never forget the Spirits who have come out to celebrate with us. Wine is poured out for them too, and we feel them right there with us. Even the dead join in, it's all life now. What fun! What an honor!

This is such a special year. In a few months, on my birthday, I will take my childhood toys to the Temple of Artemis and my new life as a young woman will really begin. Who knows, I may even be married by next *Anthesteria*. I hope he will be one of the good-looking young men who managed to win at the *Askliosmos* at the Solstice. Wouldn't it be wonderful if it would be Gregorios or Yanni, the handsome ones?

* * *

The Anthesteria

The *Anthesteria* was a three-day festival in late February, early March when the jars of new wine were opened. *Anthesteria* was the name of the month, from the verb *anthein* meaning "to flower," as the very first flowers of spring appeared after the winter's cold. Drinking contests took place, during which slaves and free men sat together as equal participants. On this day, a camaraderie honoring ones humanity in relationship to nature obliterated hierarchy and élitism. Rituals commemorated the gift of the vine. Along with festivities celebrating life, the dead, too, were said to roam freely amongst the living. The first day was also uncanny with the presence of the spirits. A procession led to the sanctuary of *Dionysos Limnaios* (from *lenos*, meaning "pressing vat," *i.e.*, the place where the wine was pressed and preserved until the completion of fermentation). Here a sacred spring ran to the Under-world. On this one day of the year, this oldest of the Dionysian sanctuaries was opened, opening up a way between the living and the dead. "The souls of the dead are called *dipsioi*, the 'thirsty ones.' They were thirsty not for water but…for wine."[36] Illness, of body or mind, was believed to often be the result of some unresolved pain (murder, improper burial, etc.) from past generations.

Plato described the problems of depression and illness as "manifest sufferings" and says that they can be traced to some "ancient cause of wrath," deeds whose reverberations still continued to be felt throughout the generations.[37] The ancestors and their deeds, from this point of view, live on in us. By assuaging their pain through specific rites, they are liberated along with the living. The spirits are assuaged, helping to ensure a peaceful, productive life for the living.[38]

On the second day, Dionysos entered the city, represented by his statue on a ship on wheels, escorted through the city, accompanied by merrymaking and an atmosphere of jokes and playful obscenities, in celebration of fertility and abundance. The ship motif connects the god with his fluidic nature, which reveals itself in the gift of the vine. In dreams, the symbolism of ship or boat often points to how we navigate the realm of emotions and also the waters of consciousness. Dionysos is at home in the realm of feeling, and in traversing the waters of the many levels of consciousness. The god in his ship was welcomed by the Archon, the king of Athens, as head of the Athenian priesthood, on its way to the sanctuary of Dionysos *Limnais* (in the marshes).[39]

---

[36] Kerényi, *Dionysos*, p. 303.

[37] W. Burkert, *Ancient Mystery Cults*, p. 24.

[38] *Constellation Therapy* is a modern-day psychotherapeutic modality developed by Bert Hellinger, a German former Episcopal priest, who worked in Africa and derived this therapeutic method from the beliefs of the Zulu tribes. It is a contemporary treatment with similar principles, i.e. healing the ancestral spirits heals the present.

[39] N. Kaltsas and A. Shapiro, (eds.) *Worshipping Women, Ritual and Reality in Ancient Athens*, p. 270.

Sex and the City

The supreme culminating event occurred on the third day with the "sacred marriage" of the Queen of Athens to Dionysos. In anticipation of this momentous event, young girls literally swung, like children, on swings. The act of swinging is a lifting up in a back and forth motion to joyous dizzying heights, a clear analogy of what was to come. Through the act of swinging, heights, depths, and heights again are experienced. Its innocence comments on the purity that accompanied the abandon of the festivities. From earth to heaven and back again, opposites join in the affirmation of life.

The City's Queen, the wife of the Athenian Archon, was accompanied to the marriage rite by fourteen mature women priestesses, the *Gerarai* (meaning "ladies of honor," and the root of our word "geriatric"). They had evoked Dionysos at fourteen altars using the contents of fourteen "mystery baskets" in preparation. We are not told why *fourteen*, but fourteen is an interesting number. It is twice the number seven, traditionally associated with nature's cyclic growth and development (seven days of the week, seven traditional planets, seven colors in the rainbow, and musical tones). Seven plus seven, *fourteen*, also represents the second cycle of seven years, *i.e.* puberty. Fourteen is half the twenty-eight day cycle of the moon, fourteen days from new moon to full and then from full to new. The body of the Egyptian Osiris, having been murdered by his brother Set, was cut into *fourteen* pieces, which were retrieved by the goddess Isis in Egyptian mythology.[40] Later, when we look at the Orphic myth, which describes the dismemberment of Dionysos, he too, was cut into *fourteen* parts. Pythagoras attributed the number *fourteen* to sacrifice. The etymology of the word "sacrifice" derives from the word *sacred*. Both Osiris and Dionysos, as sacrificed and resurrecting gods, were associated with the number *fourteen*.[41] In Christianity, there are fourteen Stations of the Cross.

[40] Gertrude Jobes, *Dictionary of Mythology, Folklore and Symbols,* Part 2, p. 1218.
[41] Gertrude Jobes, *Dictionary of Mythology, Folklore and Symbols,* Part 1, p. 605.

Returning to the day's events, at sunset, the Queen arrived at a small house called the *Boukoleion* (literally, the bull's stable), which was the Dionysian '*Holy of Holies*' on the royal estate. There she would meet and "marry" the god. It has been speculated that, either her husband, the Athenian Archon, or someone especially appointed to personify Dionysos met her there. The rite was a reenactment of the union of Dionysos' parents and also his own marriage to Ariadne, a story we will soon explore. The *Hieros Gamos* (sacred marriage) of the first lady of Athens and the god ensured the well-being and prosperity of the city in the year to come.

On the final day of the festival, the dead were honored, paralleling the pruning of the vine necessary at this time of the agricultural year. Even now, in early February, as I write, I see the vines being carefully pruned in the valley below—still work done by hand—in keeping with the age-long practices of viticulture. For new life, death is requisite. The ghosts of the dead were said to be returning to the swamps and the Underworld after sharing the celebration with the living. It was understood that in celebrating life, the dead too, must be given due respect.

* * *

Althea's Diary, morning, spring, 405 B.C.

> Dear Diary,
> I am now considered a proper young woman, having surrendered the things of childhood at the Temple of Artemis on my birthday last month. I was a bit worried that I might miss my special doll, Korinna, but I really was ready to let her go when the time came.
> This will be my first Greater Dionysia, five full days of celebration including wonderful theater, as an adult. Delia will be going with me to Chloe's house where we will watch the parade. It's the best of all. The men dressed up like sileni and satyrs, showing off those

pretend phalli and swishing their tails back and forth like they are real big shots. It always makes us practically die giggling.[42]

This afternoon we will all head up to the theater for a special treat. One of Euripides' plays will be performed for the first time. Though he died, this play is new to us as we have not yet seen it.[43] Mother and Father are very much looking forward to it, having had such great respect for him. Yanni, I hear, will play Dionysos. He is so perfect for the role: tall like a god with his dark curls and beautiful eyes. Some people say Dionysos is blonde, but I think of him always looking like Yanni. Nikias, my older brother, is part of the Chorus, making my parents very proud.

Did I tell you, dear Diary, that Alexia has been chosen to be trained as one of the god's priestesses, a Thyades? She will be heading to Delphi soon. I am wondering about my fate. Who will Mother and Father choose for me as a husband? But that is for later, now is festival and not time to worry!

Besides, maybe it will be Yanni after all. Please the gods, it might be so!

The Greater Dionysia

In the late spring, the Greater Dionysia took place. The festival was introduced into Athens following a severe plague that infected the city soon after its rejection of the gift of a statue of Dionysos from the city of Eleuthera in the northern part of Attica, bordering Boeotia, an area strongly associated with Dionysos. The plague was interpreted

---

[42] *Sileni* are mythological creatures that are half horse/half man, while *satyrs* are half goat/half man.

[43] *The Bacchae* was performed posthumously for the first time at the Greater Dionysia, in 405 BC. Either Euripides' son or nephew is thought to have directed it.

as chastisement from the god. As a result, the Athenians became unabashedly observant of Dionysian devotion.

The celebration opened with the traditional phallic parade. Escorting the effigy of the god, men playfully stomped along dressed as *satyrs* (half-goat/half-man) and *sileni* (half-horse/half-man) with tails swishing and sporting huge erect leather penises. The whole population, men, women, children, and slaves, participated with abandon in the jubilant procession through the streets of Athens to the Theater of Dionysus at the base of the Acropolis. There, the required sacrifices were made, and the theater was purified. For three days, playwrights competed in presentations of tragedy and satire. On the final day, five comedies were performed.

The Theater of Dionysos

The first actor to win a prize for his tragic performance was Thespis in 534 B.C., hence our term *thespian* as synonym for actor. His prize was a goat. The word "tragedy" originally meant "goatsong," a performance in honor of "the goat god" (though associated with other animals, the goats and bulls were Dionysos' preeminent totems). In fact, the word "satire" derives from *satyr,* goat-man creatures of the woods and constant companions of Dionysos, while "comedy" derives from *komodias,* meaning "singer in the revels." The dramatic arts in the West began with the honoring of Dionysos.

The Dionysian loosening of identity is well expressed in the actor's art. The player temporarily releases his or her ego identity and reaches towards the expression and embodiment of another. The art of the actor is the in-depth exploration of feeling and thinking, instinct and willing of another being. The range of emotional and mental coloring explored through a true actor's art and devotion to craft dips into the whole palette of human expression.

A common prop and signature of Dionysian theater was the mask. There is a modern day theatrical exercise prescribed at The

Juilliard School in New York, in which acting students are first given a blank mask, then masks depicting various emotions. Wearing the first mask, deprived of facial expression as communication, the students practice depicting personality and character through *the body*. Once again, we see the value given to the *soma* (body) in the Dionysian current. Dionysian expression took one out of the head and into the body and feeling. The masks also highlight the impermanence of identity, which could shift from one mask to another, wherein the actor loosens his own self-identity to express another human experience.

> As God of carnival, of the masquerade, he is concerned with the constant metamorphosis of identity and opposed to any fixed identification with a role. To be Dionysian, one needs not only to identify fully with the person, animal or divinity pictured by the mask but also to accept that this identification is never definitive and final.[44]

Greek tragedy and comedy enacted the agony/ecstasy paradox, exploring and celebrating the flexibility and varying range of life experience.

The Democracy of Dionysian Worship

Hearty drinking and feasting followed the performances. Prisoners and slaves were freed so they too could join in. The *Dionysia* was a liberating and "levelling" time in which hierarchies were eliminated. The tedium of day-to-day life and the separation between caste and clan dissolved in the joyous conviviality of Dionysian celebration. For a short while, the exuberance of nature obliterated the mores and manners of civilized society.

---

[44] Ginette Paris, *Pagan Grace,* p. 49-50.

Vestiges of these Dionysian festivities carry on in the Christian Mardi Gras and Jewish Purim. These celebrations serve a vital psychological need to release pent-up energy that is normally contained in organized society. A sense of common humanity, a fundamental unity irrespective of gender or class, prevails, harking back to a lost primal innocence and the underlying truth that we really are all one.

In other parts of Greece, there was a biennial cycle rather than yearly. The theme of life and death was extended to cover a two-year period with the first year being devoted to the renewal of life and the second to his presence in the Underworld. This two-year cycle emphasized not only the cycle of life and death, but also "the indestructibility of life"[45] throughout both halves of the round. Whether yearly or biennially, it should be noted that the role of women in this celebration of "indestructible life" was particularly significant, in fact crucial, in all Dionysian rites and celebrations.

In the following chapter, we will explore the sacred stories that supported these festivals and gave them meaning.

---

[45] Kerényi, *Dionysos*, p. 200.

4

Mythic Beginnings

The two most influential Dionysian myths, the Theban and the Orphic myths, will help us better understand the celebrations, rites, and mysteries in honor of the god. The Theban myth is related to his popular worship in both urban and rural contexts, while the Orphic underlies initiation into his sacred mysteries. In both, we find conjunctions between mortal and immortal. Desire prompts a union that has far-reaching consequences, implying that something new—a greater potential—is possible when the terrestrial is seeded with the Divine.

The Theban Myth—Parents and Politics on Parnassus

The story begins with the lovely princess of Thebes, Semele. Her father was the mortal Cadmus, the hero-king of Thebes. Her mother Harmonia was the goddess who was said to preserve both marital and political harmony. She was the granddaughter of Poseidon on her father's side and the great-granddaughter of Aphrodite and Aries on her mother's.

The great god of gods, Zeus, became enamored with the beautiful maiden. When Zeus' wife, Hera, discovers their union, she is infuriated. Disguised as an old woman, she cunningly wins Semele's trust. When Semele confides that her lover is actually the great god, Zeus, Hera manages to sow seeds of doubt. She convinces her to ask her divine suitor to prove his identity by appearing in all of his glory.

Alchemy of the Heart

Though loathe to comply, Zeus must, because he has already taken an oath by the River Styx to give Semele anything she desires. Even the greatest of the gods must abide by an oath. He arrives at her bedchamber in a chariot amidst thunder and lightning, revealed fully as the god he is. His brilliance is far too great for human eyes and sensibilities and Semele is instantly incinerated. However, at that very moment, Zeus retrieves the young fetus of their child from her womb and implants it in his thigh. (Symbolically, the thigh is a euphemism for testes, the male generative equivalent of the womb).

Semele was six months pregnant at the time. Thus, Dionysos was incubated by his mother for two-thirds of his gestation and one-third by his father. No other god had a human mother, and no other member of the pantheon besides Athena is born from a father.

> ...the myth of his birth...is the most sublime expression of his Being. Just as the amazing image of Athena's ascent from the head of her father can be conceived only in the spirit of the genuine revelation of her Being, so beneath the lightning flashes of Dionysus grew the certainty that the enigmatic god, the spirit of a dual nature and of paradox, had a human mother and therefore, was already by his birth of two realms.[46]

Dionysos holds a unique position among gods and men, not only being of mixed divine and human parentage but also gestated by both mother and father.

In Apollodorus' version of the myth, Zeus gives the child to Hermes, who brings him to Semele's sister Ino and her husband, Athamus, the king of Boeotia. Hoping to protect Dionysos' identity from Hera, Hermes instructs the couple to raise Dionysos as a girl. "This apparent 'girl with the heart of a boy' grew in loveliness and

---

[46] Walter F. Otto, *Dionysos: Myth and Cult*, p. 73.

strength until he was ready to go search for his lost mother."[47] However, Hera discovers the ruse and curses the foster couple with madness.

Hermes, another god of the in-between and liminality, intervenes to save Dionysos, taking him to the nymphs of Nysa, which is said to have been somewhere in Asia. The young god soon discovers the gift of the vine. However, Hera at last succeeds in her goal to discover his whereabouts and drives him mad. He wanders down into Egypt and then to Syria. There, the daughter of Gaia, the Great Mother goddess, Rhea/Cybele, takes pity. She cures him and then initiates him into her sacred mysteries.[48]

Healed and initiated by Rhea, the goddess of nature's wildness, Dionysos is a masculine god in deep rapport with the earth and the feminine. A god who is not limited to any one world, he is not only familiar ("family") with the Middle World of humanity, with the Upper World of the gods, with both masculine and feminine but also with the Underworld. Later in his story, we find him travelling down into Hades to meet and save Semele, the mother he has never known. Bringing her to Olympus, she is given divine status. Even the Orphic myth, which teaches that Persephone, the goddess of the Underworld and she who brings spring each year, is his *true* mother, confirms his familiarity with the depths as well as the heights and the in-between. Each element of this myth serves to define Dionysos as a god who transcends boundaries, one who can cross thresholds and who mediates and conjoins opposites.

Cured, Dionysos returns to Semele's homeland, Thebes. Tragedy ensues as a result of the arrogance of King Pentheus, his cousin, who denies him and persecutes his followers. The story is preserved in the play, *The Bacchae,* written by Euripides in the late 5th century B.C. for the largest of the cyclic Dionysian festivals, the *Greater Dionysia.*

---

[47] Nor Hall, "Those Women," from *Dreaming in Red*, p. 180.

[48] Apollodorus, *The Library of Greek Mythology,* p. 101, 102.

Dionysos inflicts madness (what we would diagnose as mania and psychosis) on Pentheus and those in the court who have mocked and denied him. At first, the effect is comical, 'but ultimately' the dishonor of the god has gruesome and devastating consequences. The very same punishment he received from Hera, madness, is the retribution he administers. The pathologies (*pathos*, literally meaning "suffering") associated with Dionysos are the heights and depths of mood disorders as well as the delusions, and sometimes even the hallucinations, of psychosis, as well as addictions of all varieties. Dionysos' own early fate becomes the punishment of those who mock and deny him. In contrast, those who honor him experience exaltation and joy. The energetic patterns in the ancient world experienced and described as "gods" have their healthy, life-enhancing, invigorating expression, and when misused, their death-dealing destructiveness.

The Orphic Myths—Orphism and Dionysos

Orphism sprung from the legend of Orpheus, the most renowned and beloved Greek poet and musician. The earliest surviving reference to Orpheus is a fragment of a sixth century B.C. lyric poet, Ibycus, which reads, "Orpheus, of famous name."[49] It is speculated that Orpheus may have been a real person who lived in Thrace before the end of the Athenian Kingdom (c. 800 B.C.), and perhaps as early as the time just prior to the Trojan War (ca. 1300 B.C.).[50] In Apollodorus, we read that Orpheus was the son of Apollo and Calliope. He "practiced the art of singing to the lyre, and set rocks and trees in motion by his singing."[51] He was a seer and a magician and is credited with having

---

[49] W.K.C. Guthrie, *Orpheus and Greek Religion*, p. 1.

[50] Guthrie, *Orpheus and Greek Religion*, p. 1.

[51] Apollodorus, *The Library of Greek Mythology*, Book 1, Theogony, 1.3, p. 30.

introduced the sacred rites and the initiatory mysteries to Greece.[52] So great was his reputation that he was deified by the Greeks.

An essential myth associated with him relates a story of great love and loss, of courage, and ultimately failure as a result of a tragic loss of faith. It spans this life and the next, this world and the realm of the dead.

> The most famous episode in the Orpheus legend is that of his descent into the underworld…Virgil was responsible for the finest version of the myth, which is to be found at the end the *Georgics,* but this is certainly not an early version…Orpheus, we are told, had married Eurydice, daughter of a wood-nymph and Apollo…One day, when the young woman was walking by a river in Thrace, she was pursued by Aristaeus, the son of the nymph Cyrene and a river god; she ran off, but was bitten by a serpent lurking in the grass and died. Orpheus, inconsolable, determined to find his way to the underworld and bring Eurydice back to earth. The sound of his lyre charmed not only monsters guarding the approaches to the infernal world, but the gods of the dead themselves, and for an instant the damned were relieved of their torment. Hades and Persephone agreed to surrender Eurydice, but on one condition: that Orpheus must go back to the world of light, followed by his wife without once turning round to look at her before he left the kingdom of the dead. However, just as he was about to step into the light, he was afflicted with terrible doubt: had Persephone tricked him, he wondered, was Eurydice really behind him? He could not resist turning round, and saw Eurydice fade away,

---

[52] *The Hymns of Orpheus*, trans. Thomas Taylor, Sect. 1, p. 8.

dying for a second time. This time the underworld remained obstinately closed to him. Orpheus returned alone and inconsolable to the world of men.[53]

In spite of the transcendence represented by Orpheus, he too, is no stranger to the Underworld, as he courageously journeyed there in hopes of retrieving his lost love, Eurydice, from the jaws of death. His familiarity with the Underworld links him with Dionysos, who likewise made that journey to retrieve his mother, Semele, and also with the goddess, Persephone, who was abducted into the Underworld by the god Hades. In fact, Orpheus is said to have invented the mysteries of Dionysos.[54] Orpheus, like Dionysos and Persephone, has a *chthonic* (relating to the Underworld) aspect, along with his association with nature. The hymns attributed to Orpheus sing to nature imbued with divinity and to the Divine as it suffuses nature.

However, in contrast to the natural and Underworld cycle of mysteries celebrated at Eleusis, honoring Persephone and her yearly return from the Underworld to the living and her mother Demeter, the Orphic impulse was more transcendent and spiritual. How did that impulse interact with the wild soul quality of Dionysos?

> … when Orpheus tamed the animals with his music, he was taming Dionysos. He was the missionary of the wild god. A solitary wanderer, singer, musician, and writer, he wrote hymns to Dionysus, organized initiation material, and established doctrines that were beatific— and bloodless. In his hands the *thyrsus* that had been the exquisite instrument of frenzy—causing madness, inflicting injury, orchestrating the dance—became an instrument of peace and order. In the second century

---

[53] Pierre Grimal, *Larousse World Mythology*, p. 173.

[54] Apollodorus, *Library*, 1.3.2, p. 30.

A.D., we were told it was used to enforce rules of proper behavior in the meetings of Dionysian associations. If someone misbehaved, a steward, as stern and as unbending as the staff itself, set the *thyrsus* down beside the offender who understood this gesture as his signal to leave the hall. Thus, the crude, inciting stick became the refined meter of propriety, and the impulse to go wild is restrained.[55]

Orphic influence might be construed as a thinning of the rich platelets of Dionysian blood. But it might also be viewed as adding a necessarily transcendent/spiritual element to the Dionysian theme. The worlds of nature and the Underworld need the heights, just as the pure realms seek out the vitality of sap and soil of the earthy and subterranean realms.

The Orphic Dionysos Myth

In the Orphic version of the myth, Dionysos is associated with the god *Zagreus*. The name *Zagreus* comes from the Ionian word *zagre*, meaning "pit for the capture of live animals." *Zagre* is related to the root *Zoë*, the dynamic quality of life so vibrantly embodied by Dionysos.[56] Zagreus was an ancient hunting god of Crete and he was "spoken of as the highest of all the gods." This line comes from the *Alkmeonis*, an epic written in the 6th century if not earlier: "Mistress Earth and Zagreus who art above all other gods."[57] The Earth Mother is linked with the supreme god, a sort of Zeus of the Underworld.[58] And as noted,

---

[55] N. Hall, *Those Women*, from *Dreaming in Red*, p. 177.

[56] Kerényi, *Dionysos*, p. 81, 82.

[57] Kerényi, *Dionysos*, p. 83.

[58] Kerényi, *Dionysos*, p. 83.

Dionysos was associated with Hades, that "other Zeus" of classical Greek mythology.

In contrast to *Bromios*, "The Thunderer," *Zagreus* Dionysos is associated with the dark, with cool, with death, with resting, and even with mildness. He was seen as the "Tamer of Heat."[59] This duality of the god, as both Bromios and Zagreus, as both heat and coolness, refers to the cycle of the vine as well as to the wheel of life and death shared by all natural beings.

In the Orphic Dionysos myth, the god is said to have first been born of Persephone and again, much later, to Semele. Disguised as a snake, a common metaphor for primal phallic power, Zeus was said to have secretly stolen into Persephone's chamber. Zeus so favored the little son born from this union that he chose him to be his successor, god of gods, ruler of heaven.

However, Hera intervenes in this story as well. She enlists the aid of the old gods, the Titans. They lure the infant with toys and baubles, and when he raises a shiny hand mirror and curiously looks at his own reflection, they fall upon him and tear him to pieces and consume him. Quoting the Neoplatonic philosopher, Olympiodorus,

> …the Titans around him tore him to pieces and ate of his flesh. Zeus flew into a rage and slew the Titans with his lightning. From the vapor they gave off, soot formed, and from the soot, a stuff.[60]

Soot and ashes are not identical. Soot, not ashes, was the result.

In the alchemy of late antiquity the word employed for soot, *aithale*, means "sublimated vapor."[61] From this "stuff," both Dionysian and Titanic, humanity was said to have been created. Thus a sort of

---

[59] Vikki Bramshaw, *Dionysos: Exciter to Frenzy*, p. 46.

[60] Kerényi, *Dionysos*, p. 242.

[61] Kerényi, *Dionysos*, p. 242.

spiritualized substance that was Dionysos, mixing with the more brutish and primitive Titanic nature, forms the very essence of man.

The Orphic story ends with Athena, goddess of wisdom, retrieving one undamaged piece of Dionysos from the conflagration, his *heart*. Another version says she rescued his *phallos*, just as Isis did for Osiris. In either interpretation, the restoration of that which gives *life* is implied. The *heart* is associated with *love* in all of its aspects and is that organ which preserves *life* in the body. The *phallos* is the supreme indication of the life force and the carnal love that creates. The erect *phallos* also represents the awakening of Kundalini, as taught in the East, and is the god Shiva's foremost symbol. Shiva's *lingam* is worshipped not only as a "fertility symbol" but also as the emblem of the fully awakened and ecstatic, creative *life force,* rising from earth towards the cosmos. The body expresses something visceral and transcendent all at once. "Wisdom," represented by the goddess Athena, retrieves the source of *love* and *life*. The fundamental spirit of Dionysos, preserved by Athena, is distilled into an elixir, which Zeus later gives to Semele to drink. His pure essence will return as the child of Semele and Zeus.

Our Dionysian and Titanic Nature

In addition to the Dionysian, the Orphics taught that we, too, are heirs of the Titanic. What does the presence of the Titanic imply? Rafael López-Pedraza reviews an extensive amount of scholarly analysis, both ancient and modern, regarding the Titans, and comes to the conclusion that essentially the Titans represent excessive, unbound energy that often is accompanied by a sort of insolence, pride, and violence.[62] In contrast to the exuberant and unbound shared joy of the Dionysian spirit, the Titanic adds a perversion of egocentricity that vies for dominance. He quotes Carl Kerényi:

---

[62] Rafael López-Pedraza, *Dionysus in Exile,* p. 6.

> His [the Titan's] way of thinking is characterized by...
> a mentality which...implies all manner of deviousness,
> from lying and scheming to the cleverest inventions, but
> even the inventions always presuppose some deficiency
> in the trickster's mode of life. This deficiency relates the
> Titans to man and his limitations, showing them to be
> rooted in human reality.[63]

The Orphic religion centered on the idea of the admixture of unrefined brutish energies and transcendent possibility in man's intrinsic nature. López-Pedraza points out that we continue to experience the contention between these forces in ourselves and in our modern world. Every expression, whether small and personal or grand in scope, of avariciousness and wanton destruction, betrays the Titanic in our nature. It shows up in our daily lives in the many forms of gluttony and greed, in cruelty, in politics and a science that coldly objectify nature and the human being, in corporations and "super- powers" largely without conscience. It shows up in unthinkable yet very real acts of modern warfare, including the atomic bomb, and all acts of terrorism against humanity and the earth, including senseless self-destruction.

> Titanism spans a psychological spectrum [that]...is
> common in today's life: futuristic fantasies of happiness
> brought about by the ultimate technological develop-
> ment going hand-in-hand with the most destructive
> evil. It is a vision of life in which there is no inwardness,
> in which people are activated only by impulses that
> come seemingly out of nowhere, expressed through a
> superficial mimesis.[64]

---

[63] Kerényi, *Prometheus,* p. 37.

[64] López-Pedraza, *Dionysus in Exile,* p. 11.

Thus it is our fate to manage within our nature the complexity and the competition of two opposing tendencies: that which stands with life and love (the Dionysian) and that which is greedy, power hungry, and ego-driven (the Titanic). The lack of self-reflection assigned to the Titans by López-Pedraza contrasts with the self-reflection symbolized by the child Dionysos' fascination with his reflection in the mirror. There is something in us that would look, that would become self-aware. And this is the part of us that struggles against the tendency for raw unconscious use of power. This capacity for self-awareness is fragile and precious.

The Orphic Dionysian Mysteries

Though we do not know with any detail the content of the mysteries associated with the Orphic myth, we do know the toys of the infant Dionysos, including and especially the mirror of self-reflection, that were featured. Universally, shock and terror and a mock death followed by an awakening/ rebirth have always been the core themes of mystery school initiation. The purpose was, and is still in many contemporary mystery schools,[65] death to an ignorance, which perceived only the physical and its limitations, and instruction of the soul about its true eternal nature and unity with the continuity of life. The following quote from *Morals and Dogma,* written by Freemason Albert Pike in the 19th century, echoes the Orphic view of Dionysos, which very likely served as the foundational philosophy of the Orphic mysteries in ancient Greece:

> ... presiding over life and death, Dionusus (Dionysos) is in the highest sense *the* LIBERATOR: since, like Osiris, he frees the soul, and guides it in its migrations

---

[65] Masonic and Rosicrucian orders are present-day Western mystery schools of initiation whose rites continue this theme.

beyond the grave...and exalting and perfecting its nature though the purifying discipline of the Mysteries... All soul is part of the Universal Soul, whose totality is Dionusus; and it is therefore he who, as Spirit of Spirits, leads back the vagrant spirit to its home, and accompanies it through the purifying processes, both real and symbolical, of its earthly transit. He is therefore emphatically the *Mystes* or Hierophant, the great Spiritual Mediator of Greek Religion.[66]

A number of thin plates of gold incised with Orphic verses have been found lying with skeletons, which give instructions on how to navigate the passage from this world to the next.[67] The oldest was discovered in the burial of a woman in Hipponion in southern Italy and is dated c. 400 BC:

This is sacred to Memory, when you are about to die, you will find yourself at the House of Hades; on the right there is a spring, by which stands a white cypress. Descending there, the souls of the dead seek refreshment. Do not even approach this spring; beyond you will find from the Pool of Memory cool water flowing; there are guards before it, who will ask you with cool penetration what you seek from the shades of murky Hades. Say: "I am a son of earth and star-filled Heaven, I am dry with thirst and dying; but give me swiftly cool water flowing from the Pool of Memory." And they will take pity on you by the will of the Queen of the Underworld; and they will give you water to drink from the Pool of Memory; and moreover you will go on the great

[66] A. Pike, *Morals and Dogma of the Ancient and Accepted Scottish Rite of Freemasonry*, p. 393.
[67] Guthrie, *Orpheus and Greek Religion*, p. 171-176.

Sacred Way along which the other famed mystai (initiates) and bakkhoi make their way.[68]

"Memory," Mnemosyne, a Titan daughter of Rhea and Uranus, and mother of the nine muses, is far larger and deeper than day-to-day memory. It has to do with what we might call *"consciousness,"* as opposed to the waters first mentioned, the waters of forgetfulness, i.e., "unconsciousness." An initiate and a Bacchante (same as Bacchantes or *bakkhoi* above) would be able to go on "The Sacred Way" because their memory/consciousness had been re-awakened. The mystery rites were rituals meant to awaken the memory of the soul to its true identity as child of the stars (part god) as well as child of the earth (Titanic), to its history and to its destiny.

Orphism was a sort of "white tantric" worship of the god. The tantric goal, as expressed in Hinduism and Buddhism, is the marriage of opposites for the purpose of transformation. White tantra, as practiced by Tibetan Buddhists and some schools of Hinduism, seeks to bring Spirit into communion with matter so utterly that transformation and illumination of consciousness result. The significant pair of opposites in Orphism are expressed as the Dionysian and the Titanic within human nature.

In absolute contrast to the intense immersion in the instinctual life forces of nature we will explore in the Maenadic expression of Dionysian worship, Orphic devotees were ascetics, who abstained from sacrificing or eating animal flesh and the wearing of wool.[69] Both sides of the spectrum found their place in the worship of the god of life, death, transformation and transcendence. The Orphic mysteries cultivated awe in contemplation of the divine life force in Nature and an expanded awareness of what Kerényi has called *the indestructible life*

---

[68] Text on Gold Foil found in Hipponion (c. 400 BC), H. Bowden, *Mystery Cults of the Ancient World*, p. 148.

[69] Guthrie, *Orpheus and Greek Religion,* p. 16-17.

through an experiential, spiritually-centered initiatory process. With the Orphics, the mystical entered the soul-and body-focused rites honoring Dionysos.

In the next chapter, we will explore the unique relationship Dionysos had to women—to feminine psychology, and to spirituality. We begin before the arrival of the Orphics, with the *Maenads*, the wild women devoted to the god, and the *Thyades,* his priestesses.

5

THE GOD OF WOMEN

Dionysos is a god accompanied and loved by women. As a child, he is attended by the nymphs, "the divine women of moisture."[70] He is cured from the madness inflicted by Hera and initiated into the mysteries of the Great Earth Mother. In Greece, we find his rites are tended by the *Gerarai*, "the ladies of honor" in Athens, and his most ardent and loyal devotees were the *Maenads* and his priestesses, the *Thyades*.

The Maenads

The *Maenads* were women who celebrated their freedom from the constraints of men and society in their worship. Possessed by their god, Dionysos, as *Zoë* itself, they cultivated a state of ecstatic consciousness and, one might say, possession by *Zoë*.

The description of the *thiasos* (the retinue of Dionysos) in the *Bacchae* gives a multi-faceted image of the woman who becomes a maenad…Whether the maenad be maidenly or matronly, the important fact is the ability to let down or let go. Little girls do not follow. Those who do are of age to "attend the rites of maturity": women in the middle stage, not pre-pubescent and not the old ones, but those in between who most intensely feel the body's demand to respond to Dionysos…

---

[70] Otto, *Dionysus: Myth and Cult,* p. 172.

Women's response to the call does not produce children; it does not serve the family in any way... she does it because it is necessary. Like Persephone, when she reaches for the narcissus flower called in the myth "the lovely toy," she is seriously toying with death.[71]

The borders of life and death dissolve in their state of at-one-ment with the god, making them capable of extraordinary feats. The division between the human and natural worlds is dissolved. As conduits of the god's energy, they become "enthused" (from the Greek *enthous* meaning "possessed by a god") and divinely mad. From all reports, this madness could be dangerous and at times bordered on death.

The celebration of the god included the *orgia*. The word *orgia* originates in the Greek verb *organ* meaning "to be aroused," "run riot," "to be in heat."[72] The *Maenads* experienced complete arousal to the god. They became one with nature, wild and untamed; however, it is imperative to understand that this was not in a lewd or lascivious manner. Rather, their wildness was profoundly reverent. Later, with the introduction of the Orphic influence, we find "*Orgia* are not "orgies," but acts of devotion stemming from the same root as *ergon*, "things done in a meaningful manner."[73] Our contemporary, profane understanding of the word "orgy" is impoverished in either case by comparison.

The *Maenads* were known for supernatural feats. They were said to run for miles barefoot in the snow, snake-charm, and suckle animal young. They were also rumored to tear wild animals and even humans apart, limb from limb, and eat raw flesh. The descriptions, written not

---

[71] Nor Hall, *Those Women,* p. 29-30.

[72] Arthur Evans, *The God of Ecstasy: Sex-Roles and the Madness of Dionysos,* p. 70.

[73] N. Hall, Those Women, from *Dreaming in Red,* p. 178.

surprisingly by men, are quite terrifying. Instinct, untempered by social constraints, can be and most likely was savage at times. James Hillman, however, takes the view that the gory characteristics are overrated. He advised an *imaginal* understanding rather than a literal interpretation.[74] Though we run the risk of overly sanitizing the intensity of the Dionysian, his point of view has its value. Rather than repulsion at the descriptions, if we look deeper to the psychic meaning, *life* experienced at its peak is always on the edge of death. In French, the ecstatic climax of orgasm is called *le petit mort*, "the little death."

The description of "raw meat" signifies the natural and primitive, in contrast to the civilized world. Alan Bleakley connects raw meat with the raw womb at menstruation and women's dreams of raw meat during that time of the month. "Uncooked meat," he writes, "represents the inner, raw and explosive qualities of woman repressed by outside convention." The womb, too, is "... raw... red raw" at this time.[75] The Dionysian aspect then, has more to do with wildness and the dark power of woman at her period than her 'light' fertile aspect. In her fertile phase, she is part of the world of men. As potential mother, woman has a socially condoned role. But as a bleeding woman, notoriously, she has been feared and often set apart from her social community. The traditional menstrual huts in tribal Africa, her exclusion from participation in communal ceremony in many Native American tribes, and the laws of Nidah (laws of purity) still practiced today by Orthodox Jewry bear witness, at least in their patriarchal interpretations. It is possible that women in earlier pre-patriarchal times actually *chose* to remain apart just as the *Maenads* did. In any case, the menstrual time is a time set apart in ancient societies when women experienced their "rawness." It was a time in which a woman's power was felt and used not for men's purposes but for her own, and in

---

[74] James Hillman, *The Myth of Analysis*, p. 276-277.

[75] Alan Bleakley, *Fruits of the Moon Tree: The Medicine Wheel and Transpersonal Psychology*, p. 271.

the service of nature. Perhaps what is especially significant is that women were universally recognized by everyone as extraordinarily powerful during their "raw" time, whether it be menstruation or when honoring the untamed god of nature.

How profoundly unfortunate that the only remnants of this understanding are ones which patronize women or interpret them as somehow "unclean" during their menses. Contemporary modern women are nearly universally denied this understanding and instead encouraged to "medicate" for "PMS" (hardly a sacred or empowering diagnosis) by a patriarchal medical establishment!

The god of women, Dionysos himself, embodies nature outside society in its awesome power and beauty as well as its awful brutality. His power was also woman's power—the power of the Earth Mother, which she bestowed upon him through initiation, and as her lover. He is not afraid of women in their power but in fact encourages them. This is not an antiseptic god for the squeamish. As a mother suffers true life-and-death passion in giving birth to her child—a child drenched in blood—so, too, Dionysos' nature is life in death and death in life, bloody and raw.

The Thyades

On the slightly tamer side were the official priestesses at Delphi, the *Thyades*. But even they were known for extraordinary physical feats.

Delphi lies on the southern slopes of Mount Parnassus with magnificent views in all directions. It was home to healing springs and a fissure in the earth, which emitted fumes said to have given second sight. Delphi was originally the home of the earth goddess, and it was said to have been protected by a monster python. Apollo killed this python and the sun god took possession of her temple. Though it came to be primarily known as the temple of Apollo and the Oracle, first it was home to the Goddess and Dionysos, deities more in tune with oracular wisdom than with the daylight consciousness associated with

Apollo. For a while, they shared this sacred space in a complementary wholeness.

As Apollo's cult gained popularity, he came to occupy many sacred sites of Dionysos and the Mother. Though her python had been defeated, the Great Mother's mysteries and power remained in the form of oracular fumes, as well as a priestess (*Pythia*) chosen to serve as the most famous oracle of the Western world, and by the Dionysian priestesses, the *Thyades*.

Dionysos and Apollo shared holy ground. The *Thyades* performed ecstatic dances in honor of Dionysos. Art depictions show the women dancing with heads thrown back, carrying timbrels, tambourines and pipes, and carrying the *thyrsus* (the traditional staff of Dionysos made of a fennel stalk and topped with a pine cone). They appear to lose themselves in communion with the god.

His presence was especially felt in the winter months, when Apollo was said to vacate the temple for the north. The eastern pediment of the temple depicts Apollo and his steeds, while Dionysos and the *Thyades* illustrate the western pediment. The east, of course, faces the rising sun while the west looks towards the sun descending just as Dionysos was said to have descended into the Underworld. During winter, with its shortened days, nature awaited the return of life, which seemed to have disappeared into the Underworld. And it was Mount Parnassus to which Dionysos was said to return each year. In contrast to our modern culture, at Delphi, the two gods were originally equally honored and reconciled. Apollo represented the daylight/summer sun that shed light and clarity, while Dionysos stood for the Underworld/winter sun, activating livingness from the depths. Apollo, the god of clear thinking who at a distance "shines" and "is very much at home in the sky realm of intellect, will, and mind"[76] gave way to Dionysos, who "teaches us proximity, contact, intimacy with

---

[76] J. Shinoda Bolen, *Gods in Everyman: Archetypes That Shape Men's Lives*, p. 130.

ourselves, nature and others."[77] Even when Apollo was in attendance at Delphi, the Oracle still gathered prophecy from the subterranean fumes of the Underworld, which was Dionysos' domain. Apollo guided interpretation.[78]

Dionysos, Ariadne, and the Sacred Marriage

The myth of Dionysos and Ariadne is critical to understanding Dionysos, especially in his relationship to women.

Ariadne became the bride of Dionysos and their holy union was a profound inspiration to his feminine devotees. Not only Kerényi,[79] but other scholars as well believe Ariadne was originally the Cretan moon goddess.

> The myth and character of this Cretan goddess comes to us in a confused form. Political changes in ancient Greece were mirrored in religious shifts, and Ariadne's worshippers—the losing side of one such shift—found their native religion suppressed. In her original Minoan form, Ariadne ("very holy") was apparently a goddess worshipped exclusively by women, a goddess of the underworld and germination, a vegetation goddess much like the Greek Persephone.[80]

As we have seen, Dionysos' Western origins are thought to be pre-Indo European Cretan. His original form would most likely have been the "Lord of the Beasts," consort of the goddess. With the superimposition of the religion of the Mycenaean Greeks, Ariadne and Dionysos did not die. New stories were told. The "classical" stories of

---

[77] G. Paris, Pagan Grace: *Dionysus, Hermes and Goddess Memory in Daily Life*, p. 23.

[78] Guthrie, *Orpheus and Greek Religion*, p. 43; Kerényi, *Dionysos*, p. 232.

[79] Kerényi, *Dionysos*, p. 105-106.

[80] Patricia Monaghan, *The New Book of Goddesses and Heroines*, p. 25.

Dionysos and Ariadne come from this development. In these accounts, Ariadne is no longer a goddess. However, as a *mortal* woman, she holds perhaps deeper value for our study. She highlights the transformation possible for *all* women.

The Myth of Dionysos and Ariadne

Ariadne was the beautiful daughter of the most powerful man in the Aegean, King Minos of Crete. Our story begins with the arrival of the annual tribute from Athens of seven youths and seven maidens (the number fourteen again). Ordered by King Minos, they have come to be sacrificed to the Minotaur, a ghastly half-bull/half-man creature who lives beneath Minos' palace. Among them is the young and handsome Theseus, Prince of Athens. He has volunteered for this expedition with the intention of slaying the monster once and for all.

The princess falls in love with him, and secretly, in defiance of her father, she offers to help him. She gives him a sword and a clew of thread. The sword will kill the beast; the thread will be used to mark his passage through the dark passageways, allowing him to retrace his steps after the deed is done. Theseus is successful. Ariadne, leaving home, family, friends and country, joins him and his comrades escaping Crete and sailing for Athens. Terrified, yet strengthened and encouraged by love, Ariadne sacrifices all security, trusting in her heart and her lover.

On the way, the ship stops on the island of Naxos. Ariadne falls asleep on the shore and when she wakes she sees the ship sailing off without her. The unthinkable has transpired. Devastated, Ariadne is abandoned and alone. The lover for whom she had defied her father, and whom she had saved from certain death, has deserted her. She has given up everything and now there is nothing. Her utter sense of abandonment is expressed in Richard Strauss' opera, *Ariadne auf Naxos*. She laments, "I will never love again, and therefore in some sense, I will never live again."[81] As psychopomp of the Underworld, she had provided the solar hero Theseus with a means into and out of the dark. Betrayed, Ariadne, the Lady of the Labyrinth, experienced her own profound descent into darkness. Waking, she will no longer be the person she had been. She will be reborn through the fire of love's pain.

In the depths of mourning, Ariadne does not yet know she has been left on the island most favored by the god Dionysos. He had glimpsed her sleeping and comes for her. Some versions of the story explain that Theseus was prevailed upon to leave so that the god, Dionysos, might claim her love. She does, indeed, fall in love with him, the truly unfailing partner. Their love is her rebirth and their marriage makes her an immortal. With her second birth and the beginning of new life, her name is changed to *Aridella*, meaning *the bright, shining one*. Dionysos presents her with a jewel-studded crown as a wedding gift. This crown is later placed in the heavens and is known as the Corona Borealis. Their marriage is lasting and happy. Dionysos, the most passionate of gods, is a faithful husband (unique among the gods) to his beloved. They have many children; that is to say, their union is fertile and highly creative.

Dionysos, Spiritual Partner

This myth has rich significance, being emblematic of the sacred *inner* marriage for women. As we have seen, in Athens a symbolic marriage was re-enacted between the wife of the Archon of Athens and a representative of Dionysos during the *Anthesteria*. The *Maenads* considered Ariadne as their queen, and like her, they felt themselves to be in a spiritual sense married to the god. In later Roman times, an initiatory ritual with the theme of the *sacred marriage* of Ariadne and Dionysos is believed to have been performed in what is now known as

---

[81] Christine Downing, *The Goddess: Mythological Images of the Feminine*, p. 55.

the Villa of Mysteries in Pompeii. That ritual, which we will explore later, met women's specific psychospiritual needs.

The marriage of Ariadne and Dionysos is archetypal, and its value is as current today as it was in ancient and classical times. "Ariadne married Dionysos as her second, *spiritual* husband."[82] Her reliance on Theseus, an outer man, is transformed into a *Hieros Gamos*, the *sacred marriage*, with her inner, spiritual partner.

"Dionysos is the lover of women who have a center in themselves..."[83]

Ariadne was the model for all Dionysian women of Greece and later of Rome, and she has been described as

> ...the queen of Dionysiac women. She alone is worthy to stand at the side of Dionysus and to become the only one raised by him to immortality. This is the reason she wears the crown which the god, in his love, later transported to heaven [the Corona Borealis].[84]

What makes Ariadne worthy? Primarily it is her courage, her intelligence, her independence, her will, and her faith. These qualities make her ripe for rebirth and the initiation of a new, expanded consciousness and creative life. As we will see in her story, she risks everything for love and she is stripped bare of all societal conditioning, a requirement for the revelation of the mysteries and of the god. The false selves, all of the *personae* adopted to meet society's needs, must be relinquished in the quest for the true self and fulfillment. The world as she had known it—family and culture—have been left behind, leaving her raw, vulnerable and open. Rebirth requires a detachment of identity from the collective. It is at this moment, the moment of her

---

[82] Robert Johnson. *Ecstasy*, p. 40.
[83] Downing, *The Goddess*, p. 61.
[84] Otto, *Dionysos: Myth and Cult,* p. 182.

death both psychologically and possibly physically, that the god reveals himself to her. Now that the walls of cultural programming have fallen away, the Divine floods her consciousness changing her forever, lifting her to that which is eternal within her.

The archetype of their union resonates strongly with a need for women to be released from age-old patriarchal definitions and open themselves to personal experience of the Divine and their own true nature. Dionysos is the natural partner of the free woman. In the following section, we will explore the story as a parable for feminine *Individuation*.

Part Two

THE FEMININE PSYCHE AND
HER RELATIONSHIP TO THE MASCULINE

6

FEMININE INDIVIDUATION AND THE ANIMUS

Having recounted Ariadne's story, it is time to understand the myth from a depth-psychological perspective. The process of *Individuation*, as outlined by Carl Jung, lays the foundation for understanding how she and present-day women achieve the wholeness held out as possibility by her union with Dionysos.

Jung's Theory of Individuation

Individuation is the name Carl Jung gave to the process of becoming the distinctive "who" that you have the potential to be. Jung makes a point of distinguishing *Individuation* from the process of *Integration,* which he believed to be preliminary to *Individuation,* the quest for fully matured expression of one's essential nature. *Integration* has more to do with becoming a healthy functioning ego, whereas *Individuation* is the journey of consciousness towards a unique and transpersonal *Self. Integration* is a preliminary requirement for *Individuation.*[85]

In Jungian terminology, the *Self* brings together opposites in a healthy, and one could say, holy inner marriage. While the process of *Integration* of the personality focuses on unravelling complexes, *Individuation* is focused on the harmonious rapprochement of contraries within the psyche: the masculine and feminine aspects of personality and also between the conscious personality and the greater *Self.*

---

[85] Carl Jung, *Psychological Types*, CW, 757-762.

83

The most evident contrary in the human psyche is the opposite gender. Thus the paramount symbol of success in the *Individuation* endeavor is the alchemical symbol of the *hermaphrodite* or *androgyne*, a metaphoric image who psychologically unites both masculine and feminine in perfect symmetry, neither subjugating the other. The yin/yang symbol would be the Eastern equivalent.

> The *Self* is not only the center, but also the whole circumference which embraces both conscious and *Unconscious;* it is the center of this totality, just as the *Ego* is the center of the conscious mind.[86]

The *Self* is far bigger than our consciousness can comprehend and the most we can do is foster a positive relationship with it. Our entire psyche lies within the larger realm of the *Self*. It is enormously powerful. Jung likened it to a *daemon*, a numinous presence that overshadows and if we properly relate to it, oversees in a positive manner our development.[87] We ignore its direction to our detriment. A person who conforms to societal norms but squelches the real needs of the *Self* sickens and dies psychically. Jung, however, insists that this uniqueness should not develop in reaction and in opposition to the collectivity of humanity. Instead, true *Individuation* leads to a healthy relationship to greater humanity, serving its deepest needs in a distinct fashion.

In the Ariadne and Dionysos myth, we find a description of the steps in a woman's psychology leading towards the inner marriage, feminine *Individuation* and the growing experience of a whole *Self.*

---

[86] Jung, *CW* 12, ¶, 444. Note: *CW* refers throughout this publication to *The Collected Works of C.G. Jung.*

[87] *Numinous* is a term coined by Rudolf Otto and adopted by Carl Jung to convey the feeling of intense meaning and awe that accompany a true experience of the Holy, that intersection of the Divine with mundane life. See Rudolf Otto, *The Idea of the Holy,* p. 5-7.

The Animus

The *Animus* has been described as "the figure of man at work in a woman's psyche," while the *Anima* represents the figure of woman in a man's psyche.[88]

> Both are psychic *IMAGES*. Each is a configuration arising from a basic archetypal structure. As the fundamental forms which underlie the "feminine" aspects of man and the "masculine" aspects of woman, they are seen as *OPPOSITES*... They act as *PSYCHOPOMPI* or guides of soul and they become necessary links with creative possibilities and instruments of *INDIVIDUATION*... Among his definitions (CW 6), Jung summarized *anima/animus* as "soul-images." He later elucidated this statement by calling each the not-I.[89]

Here we have a core definition of *animus* and *anima*. However, their attributes and how they function have been hotly debated, reflecting the changing understanding of gender in our time.

Logos and Eros

Jung first identified the masculine, and by extension the *animus*, with *Logos*.

> For purely psychological reasons I have, in other of my writings, tried to equate the masculine consciousness with the concept of *Logos* and the feminine with that of *Eros*. By *Logos*, I meant discrimination, judgment, insight, and by *Eros* I meant the capacity to relate.[90]

---

[88] Andrew Samuels, Bani Shorter, Fred Plaut, *A Critical Dictionary of Jungian Analysis*, p. 23.

[89] Samuels, Shorter, Plaut, *A Critical Dictionary of Jungian Analysis*, p. 23.

[90] Jung, *Mysterium Coniunctionis*, CW 14, ¶ 224.

In his view, the most evolved expression of the masculine principle lay in its ability to reason. *Logos* is a Greek word meaning "word" or "reason." On the other hand, Jung identified the feminine with *Eros,* a principle related to love, intimacy and relatedness.

Emma Jung, in her book *Anima and Animus,* further developed this thesis by outlining four hierarchical stages of *animus* progression: *power, deed, word and meaning.* The first two express themselves in *the hero,* while the third may be seen as *the intellectual guide* and the fourth as *the wise man.*[91] For Emma Jung, these stages represented a development in consciousness.

The identification of *Logos* with the best aspects of masculinity served to devalue the instinctual and natural. Though tremendous credit is due to Jung for the realization that each sex has psychological components of the opposite gender, the values of the dominant, patriarchal culture colored his and Emma's definitions. To a great extent, the literature that followed tended to express the same bias, by emphasizing the danger of *animus possession* in women. The *animus* was to blame for prejudices, opinions, and generally faulty logic in women. Emma Jung writes,

> One of the most important ways that the *animus* expresses itself then, is in making judgments, and as it happens with judgments, so it is with thoughts in general. From within, they crowd upon the woman in already complete, irrefutable forms. Or if they come from without, she adopts them because they seem to her somehow convincing or attractive. But usually she feels no urge to think through and thus really to understand the ideas she adopts and, perhaps, even propagates further. Her underdeveloped power of discrimination results in her meeting valuable and

---

[91] Emma Jung, *Animus and Anima,* p. 3-4, italics mine.

worthless ideas with the same enthusiasm…because anything suggestive of mind impresses her enormously and exerts an uncanny influence.[92]

One might wonder how much this impression of female weak-mindedness arose as a simple fact of the discrepancy in education offered to men and women of the time. One might also wonder how Emma could trust her own ideas on the matter, seeing that she was a woman. In any case, while men were highly encouraged by Jung and his wife to contact and integrate their *anima*, the greater part of the *animus* literature concentrated on the danger the *animus* posed to the feminine ego.

> In analytic jargon, the *anima*—except in the case of *anima* possession– is accorded respect, even reverence. The concept of the *animus* is often used to disqualify a woman's accomplishment: "She just had a good *animus*." Such an expression means that a woman has lost a great deal of the "feminine." When the word *animus* is used, a value judgment–"That should not be"– easily creeps in… yet it is precisely the concept of the *animus* that gives a woman the possibility of living her inherent "masculine" characteristics and thereby gaining more autonomy.[93]

In a further illustration of this attitude, the renowned Jungian analyst Jane Hollister Wheelwright entitled the second chapter of her book *For Women Growing Older*, "How to Live One's *Animus* Without Being Caught by It."

---

[92] Emma Jung, *Animus and Anima*, p. 15.

[93] Verena Kast, *The Nature of Loving: Patterns of Human Relationship*, p. 89.

Thinking and Feeling

"Thinking" tended to be associated with the masculine, while "feeling" was confused with the feminine. In studying Jung's theory of typology, it is evident that this equation is faulty. *Feeling* and *Thinking* are psychic *functions* **not** determined by gender. However, in a patriarchal society, the fishbowl in which everyone has been swimming for quite a long time, it is clear how these concepts became entangled and confused. The definition of *Logos* and thinking as masculine and *Eros* and feeling as feminine is untenable when examined carefully. James Hillman clarifies,

> As an archetypal dominant, *Eros* differs both from the *anima* as psychological complex and from feeling as a psychological function, even if both may take on shades of *Eros* and come under its sway in that *Eros* is meta-psychological…a wider category than either *anima* or feeling… *Anima* by definition is the feminine aspect of the masculine psyche and is always feminine. *Eros*, however, is masculine.[94]

Dionysos, an Erotic Animus

Dionysos is the masculine as *lover, not* intellectual or spiritual mentor. He is sexual. "That Dionysos is the god of women means that he is masculinity, male sexuality as women experience it."[95] And he is male sexuality, as women *want* to experience it, a virile force that honors the beauty of the feminine soul through her body. In other words, he is the *erotic animus*. He does not fit into the analyst Edward Whitmont's *Logic* definitions of the masculine, which include *Father,*

---

[94] James Hillman, *Jung's Typology,* p. 87.
[95] Downing, *The Goddess,* p. 61.

Puer, Hero, and *Wise Man.*[96] Though he may come close to the *Puer* [the eternal youth] as described by Whitmont, he has more substance and depth. As the quality of *Eros* was mistakenly identified as solely "feminine," so too were the other Dionysian attributes.

Femininity came to be associated with devalued and thus repressed elements. Darkness, irrationality, emotionality and even our physical nature, seen as inferior and threatening, became synonymous with woman. James Hillman points to the classical interpretation of the biblical creation story as the root of misogyny in our *Logos*-oriented culture.

> The psychological history of the male-female relation-ship in our civilization may be seen as a series of footnotes to the tale of Adam and Eve…As long as the physical represents the feminine, the physical will go on receiving anti-feminine projections…the material aspect of the feminine, "her human body, the thing most prone to gross material corruption," will have a *doubly* negative cast. The more female the material, the more will it be evil; the more materialized the female, the more it will be dark. Upon the physical body of the feminine the fantasies of female inferiority become most florid, since just here "the abysmal side of bodily man with his animal passions and instinctual nature" is constellated.[97]

This is to say that men have rejected not only the feminine side of things, but also their *own* erotic and bodily natures as well. Woman in her self, and as carrier of this rejected masculine, has been regarded as inferior and even essentially "sinful." The witch persecutions throughout history, particularly the Inquisition, bear testimony.

---

[96] Edward Whitmont, *The Symbolic Quest*, p. 207.

[97] James Hillman, *The Myth of Analysis*, p. 219.

Bodily Definitions of Masculine and Feminine

In an effort to understand the essential definitions of the feminine and masculine, free of culture stereotypes, Jane Hollister Wheelwright looked to the female and male body. For her, feminine and masculine natures are different, not exclusive. Both think and feel but do so differently due to fundamental biological distinctions. In her words, to effect life, a woman *is,* while a man *does.* A woman's anatomy is a containment rendering "a woman as independent as a man who actively asserts himself."[98] A woman, through her body, is intrinsically involved in the life process, as demonstrated by menstruation, gestation, and giving birth. The man, on the other hand, has to act in order to be involved. The feminine in this primal view might be seen as the creative cauldron of the potentiality of life. From her, life takes form. The masculine can be envisioned as the directed energy, which serves to focus and inform the creative potential.

Irene Claremont de Castillejo also takes the view that the feminine is the source. Women, unlike men, are never separated from this source. To Castillejo, the *animus* helps a woman to express her soul. The *animus* functions as a torch to "light up for her the things which she already innately knows, so that she can know she knows them."[99]

In order to get a reliable reading of the masculine principle and experience of body, it is best to look to a male author. Eugene Monick argues the nature of *phallos* is indicative of primary "maleness."

> To write of archetypal masculinity means to concentrate upon phallos, the erect penis, the emblem and standard of maleness. All images through which masculinity is defined have phallos as their reference. Sinew, determination, effectuality, penetration, straight forwardness,

---

[98] J.H. Wheelwright, *Women and Men*, p. 9.
[99] I. Claremont de Castillejo, *Knowing Woman*, p. 84.

hardness, strength—all have phallos giving them effect…
Erection points to a powerful inner reality at work in a
man, not altogether in his control. The inner reality may
be different from a man's conscious desires at a given
time. Phallos is subjective authority for a male…This is
what makes phallos archetypal. No male has to learn
phallos. It presents itself to him as a god does.[100]

Phallos and Animus

Monick divides *phallos* into solar and chthonic expressions.
Further, each has a light (conscious) and shadow (repressed, unconscious) aspect. The chthonic, or earthy expression of *phallos,* is *not*
to be confused with shadow or evil.

Solar Phallos

Solar phallos, as Monick describes it, is represented by the god
Apollo. Qualities associated with *solar phallos* are the bright "light" of
reason, intellectual acumen, visible heroic effort. The masculine ideal
of reaching the top, whether it be the academic or corporate ladder or
Mount Everest, is *solar logos* activity. In its highest manifestation, *solar
phallos* is spirit. The ability to reason, to separate in order to understand,
has been a valuable contribution to human evolution. E. Monick writes,

> *Solar phallos* is the political party a man belongs to, the
> papers he reads, the alumni associations he supports,
> the legal agreements he signs, or, even, more basically,
> his word being as good as his bond. *Solar phallos* is a
> man's profession, the adequacy of his financial and

---

[100] E. Monick, *Phallos: Sacred Image of the Masculine*, p. 9.

moral support of his woman and his offspring…It is how a man speaks, what he speaks about, how he follows words with action.[101]

However, *solar phallos* has its abuses. Its shadow is present in the paternal dictatorship, which demands wife and children to be who he says they should be and in his generosity, which bears secret strings. He is active in the demeaning and humiliating way an employer or manager treats the weaker and more vulnerable. For him, principles are everything, and he will condone the slaughter of millions to preserve them. The descriptions of the dangers the *animus* poses to women mostly reflect the definition of the shadow *solar phallos*.

The Chthonic Phallos and Dionysos

Chthonic phallos is well-represented by Dionysos. *Chthonic phallos* is deep and bodily. In its positive function, it is passionate and of the earth. Its interest is the ecstasy of life, echoing our Dionysian theme.

> *Chthonic phallos* is the means by which a man moves through ego limitation to ecstatic merger with the archetypal world in sexuality. It is the numinous source of his being male. It is the silent god within, prompting creative action, standing behind his erectile strength, facilitating the explosion of his fertilizing seed. *Chthonic phallos* is the hidden source of masculine power, dark because of its hiddenness, capable of catastrophic rage, but capable also of tender love and keen attention, based upon instinctual nature and need. What happens in darkness to a male tells the story of his contact with divinity, whether that divinity be light or shadow, or a

---

[101] Monick, *Phallos*, p. 102.

mixture of both. Darkness is chthonic. Darkness is not
evil. Darkness is the home of the spark.[102]

We are all familiar with the *shadow* side of *chthonic phallos*. It
manifests itself in the cruel abuses of power in the forms of rape,
torture, murder, acts of terrorism, and the collective slaughter of war.
Repressed, the Dionysian energy becomes brutal and senselessly
destructive, as does the *chthonic phallos*. With its fearful consequences
of madness and brutal murder, Euripides' play *The Bacchae* graphically
illustrates the results of Dionysian, *chthonic phallic* repression. A
reclaiming of the positive chthonic requires a valuing and honor of the
Dionysian principle.

The *shadows* of both *chthonic* and *solar phallos* are motivated
by domination, whether physical, mental, or spiritual. Our cultural
focus on the *solar phallic (Logoic)* masculine and repression of the
chthonic has resulted in the unconscious activation of the shadow sides
of both *solar* and *chthonic phallos*. In spite of efforts made toward equal
rights, discrimination against the "darker" races, and anyone not
conforming to the *solar logos* ideal, continues as well as misogynism
and the crimes of human and environmental rape. Monick urges men
to reclaim their own positive bodily nature as well as to face both
shadows. Repression and denial create congestion in the psyche that
tends to erupt in unhealthy expression.

In his mythology, Dionysos is never dangerous unless he is
denied, in which case he finds his way back into the picture with a
vengeance. Monick argues that if men in our contemporary world
would face *shadow* and integrate *both* aspects of *phallos* in a healthy
expression, the effects would not only benefit them personally, but also
would serve to liberate women and minorities from *shadow* phallic
abuse, and raise enough concern to effect sufficient change in how we
manage Earth's resources.

---

[102] Monick, *Phallos*, p. 95.

I would add that the prevalence of addiction, too, would be addressed. Dionysos is the lord of that which alters consciousness for good, and if misused, for evil. Addiction is not limited to alcohol and drugs. It covertly sneaks into any domain, which is used to escape and numb pain. It shows up in eating disorders, in anything we do too much of, and in all of the compulsive behavior that serves to take the mind off uncomfortable emotions, including the addiction to technology. It includes even socially praised activities like work and exercise. It shows up in the perversion of the life force itself. The addiction to pornography, thanks to the Internet, is rampant and is a way *shadow chthonic phallos* insists on attention, having been denied and repressed in our culture. The Dionysian force truly is a door to the demonic if not owned and healthily expressed. And it is the portal to sacred sexuality and spiritual initiation and transformation when it is rightly honored.

Dionysos—Consort of the Embodied Feminine

> Throughout its development the Dionysian cult preserved the character it had when it first entered into history. With its sensuality and emphasis on sexual love, it presented a marked affinity to the feminine nature, and its appeal was primarily to women; it was among women that it found its most loyal supporters, its most assiduous servants, and their enthusiasm was the foundation of its power. Dionysus is a woman's god in the fullest sense of the word, the source of all woman's sensual and transcendent hopes, the center of her whole existence. It was to women that he was first revealed in his glory, and it was women who propagated his cult and brought about his triumph.[103]

---

[103] Johann Jakob Bachofen, "Introduction" to the section on "Mother Right," *Myth, Religion and Mother Right*, p. 101.

By virtue of biology, a monthly round of menstruation and the experience of pregnancy and birth, women have a heightened awareness of life and death. The inner partner, or consort, of the chthonic feminine is he who is present in pulsating life and likewise in the extinguishing of its flame. Dionysos is the *animus* of menstruating and also the menopausal or near-menopausal women, as evinced by the *Gerarai* priestesses in Athens, and the women who, in later Roman times, were initiated into his mysteries in Pompeii. Alan Bleakley writes of Dionysos and the menstruating woman,

> The 'inner flaying' of the womb is Dionysian, frenzied
> and raw, shown in the blood-rich dreams and visions,
> and the assertiveness, the threatening but proud
> *animus*-stance…that the period may bring[104]…the
> woman may meet the womanly-god as a horned god,
> who visits as an inner-animal at the period, representing
> a particularly energized aspect of her *animus*.[105]

As dark, moist god and the Underworld Sun, Dionysos is the natural partner of the menstrual goddess. When women rediscover their untamed menstrual power, and in later years, their menopausal power experienced by jolts of unexpected heat, the parallel emergence of the chthonic masculine is inevitable.

Men, too, benefit. Alan Bleakley believes that both the earthy and virginal/maternal goddesses are vital *anima* figures for men. Through them, men are able to discover the healthy expression of their own solar and chthonic power. His solar power, or god, is the Self as *heroic ego:* man in the world, father to and protector of his children. He seeks union with the *muse/lover* aspects of the goddess as inspiration.

---

[104] Bleakley, *Fruits of the Moon Tree*, p. 123.

[105] Bleakley, *Fruits of the Moon Tree*, p. 240.

However, this hero must be "rounded."[106] He must come to know his own passionate dimension and dialogue with the "menstrual *animus* energy" of woman.

The Expression of the Dionysian Animus

Jungian analyst Polly-Young Eisendrath has made a significant contribution to the understanding of the *animus* in modern women. She has assigned the Dionysos/ Ariadne myth to the fourth of five stages of *animus* development. Her five stages include: 1) *Animus* as *Alien Other*; 2) *Animus* as *Father, God and Patriarch*; 3) *Animus* as *Youth, Hero, Lover*; 4) *Animus* as *Partner Within*; and 5) *Animus* as *Androgyne*. Dionysos as the partnership aspect of *animus* activates the restoration of personal authority in a woman. Having reached this stage, a woman like Ariadne

> ...experiences herself as re-membered. She has re-covered her consciousness as a strong and competent woman and has the feeling of being reborn. What was passively acted out or projected, in terms of authority and competence in herself, is now experienced and actively pursued. She feels her own agency without oppressive concerns for approval and reflection from men or other authority figures. She is able to see herself and other women realistically in a broad social context...She turns her attention more toward embracing the "life of a woman," often by supporting other women and cherishing friendships with women and neglected aspects of herself.[107]

---

[106] Bleakley, *Fruits of the Moon Tree*, p. 14.

[107] P. Young-Eisendrath, *Hags and Heroes, a Feminist Approach to Jungian Psychotherapy with Couples*, p. 37.

In her union with Dionysos, Ariadne is wedded not to a patriarchal god but to the masculine "other," who embodies passion and ecstasy, the life force itself.

Because there is no suppression of her nature, she does not experience internal conflict when she comes into relation with the *animus* as described and cautioned by Carl and Emma Jung. The wariness with which traditional Jungian psychology has approached the *animus* is no longer necessary. The terms *anima* and *animus* derive from the Latin, *animare*, means "to enliven." Dionysos, as a chthonic *animus* figure functions as "the enlivener" *par excellence*. He serves to inspire wonderment at life's and death's processes rather than the detachment of the one-sided solar viewpoint which anesthetizes in its distance.

Dionysos as Androgyne

Though Young-Eisendrath's model does not attribute a myth to the fifth stage of *animus* as *androgyne*, I believe it is the second part of the Dionysian story. He is lover, faithful partner, and the other half of the androgyne to Ariadne. He is androgyne and she achieves a positive androgyny—wholeness—through him. Dionysos was considered both virile masculine and feminine. His femininity arises in, and as a response to, the feminine within his own nature. Because he loves the feminine, the feminine deeply responds to him. What a contrast with the stories relating to Apollo:

> Remember the chases of Apollo and the fleeing maidens. Is not their flight continuing in the *anima* reactions of Apollonic consciousness? In contrast to Apollo's failures with conjunction, Dionysos attracts the feminine, drawing it forth like sap in plants, the wine, and the milk that flows at birth.[108]

---

[108] J. Hillman, *The Myth of Analysis*, p. 286-287.

Dionysos is a fully masculine god, and is also feminine in that he is vitally in touch with the feminine within and without. In Ariadne and Dionysos, a wholeness is lived together and also when they are apart. Ariadne, who had been mistress of the dark regions of the labyrinth, has transformed and become Aridella, "she who has become clear."[109] She embodies the clarity that comes from the experience of the depths and who has had the courage to live her nature and her truth. Through her marriage to Dionysos, her own phallic nature is revealed and integrated. She is a self-realized woman.

The Whole Woman

When a woman reaches this stage, she is not a masculinized woman. Striving to be a poor copy of a man is simply perpetrating the negative solar phallic agenda. Rather, she experiences herself as woman, whole and complete. She does not experience loneliness or neediness as do less evolved women. She is not defined by her relationships. Yet she is also deeply and authentically engaged with others. She has found her voice and even if she experiences self-doubt or uncertainty from time to time, she does not allow those doubts to silence her. She has a connection with internal resources and wisdom with which she finds guidance and reassurance. She feels the support of the internal masculine wedded to her soul. She is comfortable in the company of women, and of men, knowing in her bones who she is. In the following chapter, we will explore essential contrasting images of the sacred feminine and take an even deeper journey into the story of Ariadne.

---

[109] Linda Fierz-David, *Women's Dionysian Initiation*, p. 127.

7

THE SACRED FEMININE

In the last two thousand years, the nurturing aspect of *Mother* has been the only universally accepted expression of the sacred feminine in Western culture. We find her embodied in the Virgin Mary—the Christian model of the ideal feminine, and in the *Shekhinah* of Jewish tradition.

Mary, the Shekhinah, and Lilith

The classic fair-skinned Christian Madonna is the feminine counterpart to the solar phallic principle dominant in our culture. Alan Bleakley calls her the *White Goddess*.[110] As the Virgin Mary, she is "handmaid of the Lord." Even the Holy Spirit of the Christian Trinity, which could and should easily be associated with the feminine (the Hebrew word for "Spirit" is the *feminine* noun, *Ruach),* is traditionally addressed as *He.* Judeo-Christianity has never accorded her entirely equal rank to the male deity. Conspicuously missing in common observance, as well, are the *Shekhinah* of Judaism (considered the feminine presence of God), as well as the dark lunar figure of Judaism, Lilith.

The "light" expression of the Divine Mother—the accepted orthodox Christian feminine image—is compassion purity; humility; patience; nurturance; devotion; gentleness; quiet strength and wisdom. Her *shadow,* however, is passivity and what might be interpreted as

---

[110] Bleakley, *Fruits of the Moon Tree.*

subservience. Monica Sjoo and Barbara Mor write of this *shadow* aspect of our understanding of Mary,

> Mary, the only female now left on this divine scene, has nothing of the primal creatrix about her. She is a mere, lowly, mortal woman, "lifted up" by Yahweh's divinely disembodied attention—impregnated by it, in fact, without ever seeing or touching a man—to produce a son for the heavenly father...The impregnation of Mary echoes all the classical patriarchal myths of mortal women's being implanted, by more or less force, with the seed of the Sun God.[111]

Harsh criticism. Perhaps they do not fully comprehend the value of the purity and compassion of the Marian ideal, yet their comments are shockingly and necessarily provocative, as the one-sidedness of the traditional image is incomplete and consequently repressive.

Jewish author and professor of Jewish studies at Dartmouth College, Susannah Heschel, distinguishes between the light and dark images of the feminine in Judaism:

> The polar images of mother as nourisher and smotherer in contemporary fiction parallel the twin female figures of the *Shekhinah* and Lilith found in ancient and medieval Jewish sources. Appearing in legends, mystical speculations and amulets, Lilith is a demon woman, the source of evil, temptation, and sin, who haunts the world, seducing pious men and murdering innocent babies. The *Shekhinah*, in contrast, is the gentle, loving presence of God, the daughter, queen, bride, and lover figured in prayer and prominent in Sabbath liturgy.[112]

[111] M. Sjoo, B. Mor, *The Great Cosmic Mother*, p. 350.

[112] S. Heschel, *On Being a Jewish Feminist*, p. 7.

"Then Adam came and sinned. The lines were ruined, the channels broken, the pools cut off; *Shekhinah* withdrew and the bond was severed."[113] The feminine nurturing aspect of divinity went into exile, leaving only the spiritual abstraction of "the Bride" who is said to usher in the Sabbath, the day dedicated to Lord and King.

Lilith

And who is Lilith?

> Lilith, an irresistible, long haired, she-demon of the night, flies through Sumerian, Babylonian, Assyrian, Canaanite, Persian, Hebrew, Arabic, and Teutonic mythology…a night demon who lays hold of men and women who sleep alone, causing erotic dreams and nocturnal orgasm. By the eighth century B.C. in Syria, Lilith, the succubus, was joined to what had originally been a quite distinct demonic figure of the child killing witch Lamashtu. In this form, Lilith, Winged One and Stranglers, became known throughout the world by the appellations Dame Donkey Legs, Vixen Bogey, Blood Sucker, Woman of Harlotry, Alien Woman, Impure Female, End of all Flesh, End of Day, *bruha*, *strega*, witch, hag, snatcher and enchantress.[114]

The medieval text, the *Alpha Beth Ben Sira*, gives her biography:

> God formed Lilith the first woman just as He had formed Adam except that he used filth and impure sediment instead of dust or earth. Adam and Lilith never found peace together. She disagreed with him in

---

[113] D.C. Matt, Trans., *The Zohar*, p. 216.

[114] B. Black Koltuv, *The Book of Lilith*, Introduction.

many matters, and refused to lie beneath him in sexual intercourse, basing her claim for equality on the fact that each had been created from earth. When Lilith saw that Adam would overpower her, she uttered the ineffable name of God and flew up into the air of the world. Eventually, she dwelt in a cave in the desert on the shores of the Red Sea. There she engaged in un-bridled promiscuity, consorted with lascivious demons, and gave birth to hundreds of *Lilim* or demonic babies, daily.[115]

The Zohar, or *Book of Splendor,* is a compilation of extensive mystical commentaries on the Hebrew Bible. In it we find a number of *midrashim* (Biblical commentaries) concerning Lilith, including the legend recounting that the sun and moon were originally the same size and carried their own light. But they had difficulty getting along, so God chose to diminish the moon as a way to settle the quarrel. It is said, "from that time she has had no light of her own, but derives her light from the Sun."[116] According to the Zohar, "Lilith's energy is derived from the resentment and diminishment of the moon."[117] A patriarchal god decides always in the favor of the male and understandably, her fate, experienced as a devastating injustice, results in unresolved, bitter resentment and alienation. For an in-depth understanding of Lilith, Barbara Black Koltuv's book is highly recommended. To sum up, in her words,

> Lilith is that part of the Great Goddess that has been rejected and cast out in post Biblical times. She represents the qualities of the feminine Self that the

---

[115] B. Black Koltuv, *Book of Lilth*, p. 19-20.

[116] Black Koltuv, *Book of Lilith*, p. 2.

[117] Black Koltuv, *Book of Lilith*, p. 4.

Shekhina alone does not carry. The first of these qualities is lunar consciousness, which is a reconnection to the cycles of waxing and waning: life, death, and rebirth; and the Goddess as maiden, mother, and crone… The second rejected quality…is the body— instinctually, and sexuality. In patriarchal times, woman is seen as vessel and mother, her sexuality is limited to the proscribed marital embrace, or idealized and spiritualized into Virgin…Lilith is neither. She is whore and earth. Her sexuality belongs to herself and to the Goddess…Third, both Lilith and the Shekhina represent the rejected Goddess' quality of prophetic inner knowledge and experience over logic or law…and the fourth and final feminine quality carried by Lilith is that of God the mother and creatrix, in addition to God the father and creator, in this sense, Lilith is *Adamah*, the feminine red mother earth of woman's nature…[118]

Lilith *is* insubordination *and* she is the inner flame of a woman's heroism, akin to our Ariadne.

While Lilith carries the brunt of the projection of feminine shadow, even the *Shekhinah* is perceived by some with fear. An Israeli Yemenite woman whom I befriended in a class in Jewish Kabbalistic studies described to me an actual terror imprinted in childhood of the *Shekhinah*. As an adult, she acknowledged the *Shekhinah* as a feminine side of God, but still perceived her as primarily dangerous and unapproachable. Apparently, in the culture that surrounded my friend as a child in a Yemenite community in Tel Aviv, not only Lilith, but the *Shekhinah,* too, was believed to be destructive and even frightening, a power really from which to steer clear. Perhaps there was a conflation

---

[118] Black Koltuv, *Book of Lilith*, p. 122.

in the minds of the common people of these two feminine archetypes in Judaism, leaving really only the bare abstraction of the "Sabbath Bride" and "God the Father" as acceptable and somewhat approachable images of the Divine.

The Dark Feminine in Christianity

The dark or *Black Goddess,* symbolic of women's deep, earthy and some might say, witchy, menstrual power, has not only been exiled, but rejected. Please understand this discussion not in terms of race but in the language of symbolic metaphor.

Her "shadow" (negative connotations), which is most familiar to Western culture, is personified by the shrew, the banshee, and the wicked witch. Terrible things have happened to women designated as "witch" by their communities and women of color have particularly suffered as a result of this degrading and dishonoring projection by dominant white patriarchal culture.

However, a trace of her footsteps lit by flickering but growing light is found in the tradition of Mary Magdalene. For most of Church history, the Magdalene has been an ambivalent figure. In Luke 8:2, we are told that she was "cured of possession by evil spirits and infirmities," and it was she "from whom seven demons had gone out." There is no direct mention that Mary Magdalene was a prostitute, yet that association has gripped the imagination of the collective imagination for most of the Church's history. Why? There is a similar association made with Tamar of the Hebrew Bible. Like Tamar, a woman associated with harlotry who is redeemed and is prophesied to be an ancestor of the coming Messiah, good things eventuate from the woman of ill repute. This aspect of woman is on the outer fringes of society, carrying the projection of body and dark powerful instinct. Yet even in patriarchal sources there are hints that from darkness emerges great light.

Recent scholarship seeks to redeem Mary Magdalene from the centuries-long blackening of her reputation. But I would argue that her blackening is archetypal, significant, and essential. Humanity, composed of body, soul, and spirit, contains the whole spectrum of experience. Life is not so easily dissected into good and evil. Great good can come from the darkest depths, and the deepest love from a passionate body and heart. If Mary Magdalene were possessed by seven demons, she was in every way (and those who hear reference to the seven chakras would agree) suffering, and far removed from a blissful state of light and grace. And her suffering and imperfections make her even more human, vulnerable and, for Christ, lovable.

Sensuality is associated with her. What is Biblically documented is that she was one of the women who brought spices to anoint the body of Jesus.[119] His body (sensual receptor) is lovingly cared for by her spiced oils (the sensual experience of fragrance). This, in fact, is documented in the Gospels.[120] What is imagined earlier in the story is that she is the woman who anointed Jesus' feet with the hugely expensive and wonderfully fragrant oil from India, called *nard*, along with her tears.[121] What a sensual demonstration of the deepest love and absolute devotion! In Mark's and Matthew's Gospels, a similar event is described, but this time an unnamed woman pours fragrant oil on the head of Jesus. All versions of the story have been attributed to Mary Magdalene, although there is no direct reference.

I believe there is a soul understanding, or comprehension, of the resonance. Devotion, passionate devotion, and oddly enough, absolute fidelity—when it finds a worthy recipient—is the gift of the

---

[119] Mark 16:1-19, NRSV edition (New Revised Standard Version), Harper Collins, NY, NY, 1989.

[120] Mark 16:1-19, NRSV edition (New Revised Standard Version), Harper Collins, NY, NY, 1989.

[121] John 12:1-8, Luke 7: 36-50, NRSV edition (New Revised Standard Version), Harper Collins, NY, NY, 1989.

dark feminine. Like Dionysos himself, who we have seen is the "dark masculine"…she, like he, is unbendingly faithful… although spurned by collective morality and ordered society. Whether in the midst of the élitist and judgmental society of a Pharisaic home, or at the foot of the cross of a convicted criminal, Mary is there. Unlike the apostle Peter, she never abandons her Beloved.

On June 10, 2016, the Vatican announced the decision by Pope Francis to elevate the commemorative day of Mary Magdalene (July 22) to a feast day, honoring the fact that, as the first eyewitness of Christ after the Resurrection, she was indeed "the apostle to the apostles." It was she who, through her steadfast love and dedication, merited the honor, and it was she who carried the news to the other apostles. This is a highly significant event signalling the long-awaited re-emergence of the feminine, which Carl Jung noted began with the dogmatization of the Feast of the Assumption of the Virgin Mary, the Blessed Mother, to be celebrated on August 15, by the Catholic Church on November 1, 1950. Carl Jung interpreted this 1950s event as the introduction of the feminine "fourth" to the masculine trinity, a beginning of a return of the divine feminine. In 1950, the first seed was planted in reintegrating the Goddess in her virginal, mother incarnation. In 2016, at last, the bodily, lover/companion aspect of the feminine has been given the first indications of rightful honoring.

A flourishing contemporary interest in Mary of Magdala demonstrates an urgent call from psyche to value and integrate in a healthy and holy manner the passionate, embodied feminine she represents. Whether she was or was not literally the mate of Jesus is *not* the issue. The significant point is that Mary Magdalene seems to have had a deep understanding of the message of Christ, and was herself love's devotion embodied. Perhaps she understood Him because her heart and soul had travelled the depths of what it is to be human, as He was said to have done, having chosen to experience fully incarnate being.

The speculation that she may have been the Bride of Christ is emblematic of a new development in the religious collective psyche. A current is entering the collective consciousness of Christianity that God may now be experienced as "Lover" and embodied with full sensory aliveness, as the mystics have always known, and not only be related to as "Father." We are moving out of a child's relationship to God into adolescence, and it is hoped this will blossom into maturity. The partner to the divine masculine is a feminine consciousness that has deeply suffered and possesses a passionate, though waylaid heart, finding at last the proper compass direction. In a sense, all of us—male and female—are 'feminine' in relationship with the Divine, as it is our task to cultivate a state of receptivity and transparency to the sacred flame deep within our own souls.

The Black Madonna

Alongside contemporary interest in Mary Magdalene has been a vitalization of interest in the Black Madonna, a Marian image with dark features found interestingly enough in primarily white environs.

What is known objectively about the phenomenon of the Black Madonnas is that they are statues, paintings, mosaics and stained-glass windows in which the Virgin Mary is purposefully colored black or dark brown. The bulk of these works of art appeared in areas where the only external racial expression was Caucasian at the time. The images rarely have an artist associated with them, and are often attributed to the handiwork of St. Luke the Evangelist…the majority of the works of art date from the fifth and sixth centuries up to the fourteenth century. Most of the images have legends and history associated with them that date between the eleventh and thirteenth centuries. They are scattered throughout Europe, with a great number of Black Madonnas in France… and along the European pilgrimage route Camino de Santiago de Compostela.[122]

Saint Luke, the evangelist to whom artistic credit has often been given, was known as a healer and his gospel describes a good many of Christ's healing miracles. The Black Madonna, often found in crypts or in hidden side altars of ancient churches, is considered the preeminent healing mother, and her shrines are often richly decorated with prayers and thanksgiving offerings for healing.

As for her appearance in unlikely settings, I have personally encountered weathered small chapels with Black Madonnas on hiking trails in the Swiss Alps, a place surely not inhabited or even frequented by persons of color. The presence of the Black Madonna speaks to something deep within the psyche, something not easily dismissed or explained on the surface.

> The Black Madonnas evolved directly from the Great Goddess…This blackness stood for the dark side of the moon, the dark, mysterious, hidden side of the female principle…Also, of course, black, especially in Egypt, symbolized the magnitude and power of the earth, which came to embody the female principle. The blacker the soil, the richer, as farmers have always known.[123]

The connection with the soil, the earth, takes us naturally to the body. The Black Madonna is "Mater"—Mother and Matter—who can mother us back to a healthy body as well as soul.

The deep significance of these images has largely remained esoteric. A common explanation given by church tour guides is that

---

[122] Stephanie Georgieff, *The Black Madonna: Mysterious Soul Companion*, p. 5.

[123] J.H. Wheelwright, *Women and Men*, p. 11.

the blackness of the images is the result of years of candle smoke. One might be curious as to why all the images in the church are not also "black."

> What does the Black Madonna's color really convey? I personally think it is more than just candle smoke at work. When we consider the wonders of the nature of a dark universe made up of over 90% dark matter, that dark matter is the cohesive substance of the universe... the symbolism of the Black Madonna becomes quite grand.[124]

Wisdom is associated with the Black Goddess, and she is also at the heart of the creative process. Jungian analyst Marion Woodman tells us she came into Europe with the Crusaders' returning with statues of Isis, which were interpreted by the Christians as Madonna images.[125] She envisions her rising significance in contemporary cultural awareness as the bridge to an entirely new era in consciousness, which she describes as 'Conscious Femininity.'

> The Black Madonna usually appears outdoors, so she's related to nature. My sense is that she has to do with consciousness in matter. We cannot go back to identifying with *mater,* unconscious matter; and there never has been an era of conscious femininity. The world has never known Conscious Mother; let alone Conscious Mature Woman. We have to connect to her because the power that drives the patriarchy, the power that is raping the earth, the power behind addictions, has to be transformed... The Black Madonna is the bridge. She is a spiritual figure in a physical body so she acts as a

---

[124] Georgieff, *The Black Madonna: Mysterious Soul Companion,* p. 45.

[125] M. Woodman, *Dancing in the Flames,* p. 28.

bridge between the head and heart. She's a wisdom figure...the deep feminine wisdom that manifests through nature, including human nature. Sophia's (the goddess of wisdom) first appearance in dreams is often as a dark goddess."[126]

Despite a patriarchal preference for the fair-skinned Mary, an undercurrent of devotion to her has never been fully expunged.

> ...the Black Madonnas are seen...as generative intimacy that humans have with the Divine...The Black Madonnas are accessible to humanity in a unique and profound way. This Divine intimacy with humanity is symbolized by the Madonnas' earthy dark appearance, the fact that they represent the Virgin Mary, but in a mystical Black gesture.[127]

Furthermore,

> Blackness can also be seen as the badge of coming through the fire, burnt with experience. One becomes refined but still alive. This refinement is also symbolic of the transformational nature of earthly life within physical bodies.[128]

The contemporary interest in the expression of the divine masculine as *lover* and in the dark feminine is a call to a conscious relationship with the best of both sides of the masculine and feminine. Ariadne, as a derivative of the moon goddess and as Lady of the Labyrinth, is a symbol of the inner realms and the Underworld. She is resonant to both the light and dark faces of the feminine. It is time we

---

[126] M. Woodman, *The Conscious Feminine*, p. 82.

[127] Woodman, *The Conscious Feminine*, p. 23.

[128] Woodman, *The Conscious Feminine*, p. 37.

repair the one-sidedness in both masculine and feminine images. This imbalance has dominated the collective psyche for far too long, resulting in a sickness of soul and earth, and an alienation from true spirituality.

The Archetype of the Labyrinth

After many centuries of dormancy, enthusiastic recognition is being given to the labyrinth, an ancient archetypal pattern dating back at least 5000 years, based on the spiral and circular formations found in nature.

Since the early 1990s, the "labyrinth movement," spearheaded by Episcopal priest Lauren Artress, has resulted in the construction of many thousands of new labyrinths. According to website of Veriditas, the organization for the promulgation of interest in the labyrinth, founded by Dr. Artress, at least 5000 labyrinths in 80 countries have been catalogued. On a pilgrimage to France, she had experienced the medieval 11-circuit labyrinth of Chartres Cathedral, the preeminent jewel of Gothic cathedrals, and had the vision (and the feet) to know that our psyches, starving for reconnection with the embodied and "en-earthed" Divine, had a tool mostly forgotten, yet hidden in plain sight.

The labyrinth long predates Christianity, but the ones typically found in Christendom were integrated into the churches dedicated to the Divine Mother during the Middle Ages. The labyrinth is a deeply feminine symbol, with its winding rather than linear paths, evocative of the uterus and digestive organs, as well as the spiraling and cyclic patterns found throughout nature.

A labyrinth is a contemplative tool navigated via the feet touching the ground. It is a meditation that literally ensouls, i.e., en-soles, the earth by means of the human foot. It can also be seen as a mandala metaphor for the inner journey into the deeper realms of the Self and the inner reality, while being supported by the constancy of the earth.

Ariadne, Lady of the Labyrinth

The labyrinth is intrinsic to our story of Ariadne and Dionysos. It is Ariadne's knowledge of the labyrinth beneath her father's palace, and her gift of thread and sword to Theseus, so that he may slay the Minotaur at its center, that begins the tale of Ariadne and Dionysos.

The labyrinth excavated under the Palace of Knossos on Crete, and thought to be the prototype of the story, is actually a maze. The difference between a maze and a labyrinth is that mazes have dead ends and possible wrong turns, while there are none in a labyrinth.[129] One cannot lose one's way in a labyrinth. Traversing a labyrinth is a "letting go" to a trusted path, rather than the journey of the maze, which requires vigilance and courageous discernment. The image depicted on ancient Cretan coins depicts a true labyrinth, not a maze, so we do not know in fact whether Theseus was imagined to have traversed a maze or a labyrinth. The question might be why would Theseus need a boule of thread in order to find his way out again if he were in a true labyrinth? Strategy, not surrender, in this case, was essential to the successful outcome. When we move into the dark passages of the psyche seeking to "clean house," we need our wits and a means of return.

Ariadne, the mistress of the subterranean labyrinth who is believed to have been originally the ancient moon goddess of Crete, knows the threading that takes one to and from the center of psyche. It is in this dark realm that confrontation with whatever is unhealthy takes place. In this case, the undigested psychic energies have been constellated in a demonic and highly dangerous form represented by the Minotaur. Thus the work of *Integration,* wherein we face our complexes and *Shadow* is best symbolized by the maze, while the labyrinth illustrates the *Individuation* journey that can follow that

---

[129] M.G. West, *Exploring the Labyrinth,* p. 4-5

preparation. When we seek the sacred at the core of our being, a letting go in trust is the right approach.

The Minotaur was the monstrous result of the greed of King Minos and his negligence in doing due diligence to his divine benefactor, Poseidon. The Minotaur represented a demonic ancestral inheritance deeply lodged within the Cretan psyche. And it represents all dangerous human missteps and hubris in relationship to the awesome and at times awful forces that circumvent the fiefdoms created by ego.

As a soul figure, Ariadne supplies what the heroic *ego* needs to take on the perilous intra-psychic journey and reemerge successfully. She supplies the thread. The feminine is traditionally considered the weaver of life, fate and destiny worldwide. Just a few examples include, among the Greeks: *Ananke*, Goddess of Fate, *Athena, Arachne, Clotho*, and *Atropos*; the Egyptian *Isis*, and *Neit*; German *Holda*, Goddess of Spinning; Baltic *Saule*, the Solstice Goddess of spinning and weaving, the Norse *Frigg* and *Bertha*; *Chih Nii* and *Chih Nu* in China; and the Native American *Grandmother Spider Woman*. With her boule of thread, Ariadne joins their ranks as the feminine mistress of life and death, a psychopomp in the soul's journey.

The Labyrinth: Soul, Spirit, and the Self

The labyrinth in Christian churches is experienced by present-day pilgrims as a spiritual meditation that promotes soulful inwardness and connection to Spirit. As one enters, there is a releasing of everyday concerns, a practice of presence and attention to the emergence of thoughts and emotions. Reaching the center is an opportunity to open and receive the transpersonal, to connect deeply with the sacred. Weaving one's way out again, the return journey integrates what has been received throughout, so that one emerges with a greater sense of spiritual balance and awareness.

From a more psychological perspective, the labyrinth is an archetypal mandala figure, and thus it is a *Self* symbol.[130] It is a spiritual journey *and* it encompasses both dark and light aspects of the psyche, the totality of the Self.

> The *Self* is not only the center but also the whole circumference which embraces both conscious and unconscious; it is the center of this totality, just as the *Ego* is the center of the conscious mind.[131]

A Critical Dictionary of Jungian Analysis further explains:

> The *Self* is an archetypal image of man's fullest potential and the unity of the personality as a whole. The *Self* as a unifying principle within the human psyche occupies the central position of authority in relation to psychological life and, therefore, the destiny of the individual… the relationship of *ego* to *Self* is a never-ending process. The process carries with it a danger of inflation unless the *Ego* is both flexible and capable of setting individual and conscious (as opposed to archetypal and unconscious) boundaries… Lest the *Self* appear to be entirely benign, Jung emphasized that it should be likened to a daemon, a determining power without conscience; ethical decisions are left to man… the *Self* can be defined as an archetypal urge to coordinate, relativize and mediate the tension of opposites.[132] (italics and capitalization mine).

---

[130] A. Samuels, B. Shorter, F. Plaut, *A Critical Dictionary of Jungian Analysis,* p. 90.

[131] Jung, *CW* 12, ¶ 444.

[132] Samuels, B. Shorter, F. Plaut, *A Critical Dictionary of Jungian Analysis*, p. 135-136.

Clearly, in our story, Theseus was not immune to *inflation* and he betrayed his soul image— his *anima*—Ariadne. He emerges having succeeded at the task, but with a hubris that permits disrespect for, and rejection and abandonment of his feminine guide.

However, we might also interpret the story from the perspective of Ariadne's own psyche. As a woman, she was able to empower her own heroic *Ego*, in the projection onto Theseus. In so doing, she achieves liberation from the tyranny of her father and the primitive state of the collective unconscious, which her home country represents. Though bereft of home and subsequently abandoned by her lover, suffering a profound psychological collapse after the initial exaltation of victory, she ultimately achieves the Sacred (inner) Marriage symbolized by union with the god/lover/husband Dionysos.

Ariadne and Her Animus

The *animus* is connected with a woman's sense of **empowerment**. The negative *animus* is disempowering, critical and denigrating, while a positive *animus* assists a woman to live her authentic being in the world. How a man treats the women closest to him in life gives insight into how he relates to his own soul. The way in which a woman experiences the men in her life expresses how she feels about her own power, i.e., does it support or abandon her? Is it trustworthy or does it fail her?

Ariadne possesses a complex alchemical template of *animus* ingredients and the possibility for cooking these ingredients to perfection, enriching her life and being. Ariadne's *animus* begins as fragments of light and extreme darkness perverted to cruelty (as represented by her father and the Minotaur). Through her courageous and faithful intention, and ultimately with the assistance of divine grace, what was flawed and ineffectual evolves into a passionate, powerful, masculine expression that supports and fulfills her. This evolved *animus*—a masculine soul figure—is embodied in the archetype Dionysos.

To understand Ariadne's story, we must look at how the *animus* is formed in a woman's psyche and the elements that contributed to its formation from her family history. For a girl, her father is the first experience of "the other." This initial and most enduring impression of the masculine forms the first imprint of *animus*. Her father's positive strengths and his care empower her, while his weaknesses, and if he is unconscious, his projections upon her of those weaknesses, form a persistent backdrop that carries over into her relationship with boys and men. Likewise, it impacts her sense of effectiveness in the world. Her brothers and other significant male figures in her environment, along with images of the masculine in her cultural milieu, further inform the image of the inner "other." In addition to these images from "nurture," the *animus* is informed by her own "nature," something "mysteriously unique to her also."[133]

Ariadne's father was king of the most important and powerful empire in the eastern Mediterranean, the island of Crete. King Minos was reputed to have been the son of the sky god Zeus, who came to his mother, the Phoenician princess Europa, in the form of a White Bull. When Minos was grown, he married Pasiphae, the daughter of Helios, the sun god. Minos was related by both birth and marriage to the sky/solar aspects of the masculine archetype (Zeus and Helios). With Pasiphae, he had three children: Phaedra, Ariadne, and Andregeos. Mythology tells us that at a certain point in his career, his sovereignty was questioned. He prayed to the sea god, Poseidon for a sign to prove his right to the throne. Poseidon answered Minos' petition with a perfect White Bull who emerged from the sea. Archetypally, the sea represents the great waters of the consciousness and unconsciousness,

---

[133] J. Hollis, *The Middle Passage: From Misery to Meaning in Midlife*, p. 46.

the origin of all manifestation. The Bull is an ancient and enduring emblem of virility and power.

> The Bull was universally worshipped as the fecundity of nature, fertility of the earth, generative and reproductive force, heat and light of the sun, luminous and impregnating force of all things. Symbolic of energy, fury, lasciviousness, life-power, lordship, virility and wealth.[134]

The appearance of a perfect White Bull emerging from the sea left no doubt that Minos was the son of Zeus, blessed by Poseidon, and the rightful ruler of Crete. Though the sign did affirm Minos' right, he corrupted his relationship to the gods and offended Poseidon by deciding to keep, rather than sacrifice (make sacred by offering back as tribute), the perfect White Bull. White is emblematic of perfection and purity.

The Bull is the symbol attributed to the astrological sign of Taurus whose key phrase is "I Have."[135] The positive attributes of Taurus are groundedness, steadiness, kindness, and gentleness. The Buddha is, in fact, reputed to have been a Taurus, and his birthday as well as his enlightenment are celebrated by Buddhists at the full moon in the month in which the sun passes through the sign of Taurus. However, unpolished qualities in a less mature manifestation include stubbornness, over-possessiveness, jealousy, and greed. These are all the unrefined traits we find in Ariadne's father. The evolved expression of Taurus is a sense of what is truly valuable and recognition of the duty to give what is owed. In her chapter on Taurus, Isabel Hickey quotes Jesus, "Render unto Caesar what belongs to Caesar and unto God what belongs to God."[136]

---

[134] G. Jobes, *Dictionary of Mythology, Folklore and Symbols, Part 1*, p. 259.

[135] I. Hickey, *Astrology, A Cosmic Science*, p. 14.

[136] Hickey, *Astrology, A Cosmic Science*, p. 14.

She points out that the tendency to acquisitiveness, the inability to give what is due, is based on fear of loss. Minos has just experienced the fear of losing his kingdom and now, having been given Poseidon's mandate, he is unable to let go and give to the god what belongs to the god. The bull's whiteness signifies a purity of values. Minos debases the gift and concretizes *values* into materialistic *valuables*.

As the Bull is the exemplar of the masculine energy of virility and fertility, the mythological relationship is logical. Minos' wife Pasiphae represents Minos' *anima*, the voice of his own soul. In betraying the god, his own soul must give due service to the archetypal forces his inflated *Ego* has slighted. Pasiphae is compelled to union with the White Bull and a freakish child is born, a bull man, the Minotaur (Mino-Taur, Minos' Bull). In order to house this monstrosity, a labyrinth is constructed beneath Minos' Palace at Knossos on Crete. This labyrinth can be seen as a metaphor for Minos' personal unconscious. Though he lives in splendor with his family above ground, beneath paces the beast created from his sin against the god. Minos himself, can be seen to represent an inflated masculine ego that is out of relationship with his own soul and with psychic forces far greater than his personal power. His family and his subjects pay a high price.

Minos' son and Ariadne's brother, Androgeus, is murdered in Athens out of jealousy after having won all of the athletic competitions. Minos in retaliation attacks and conquers Athens and decrees a terrible penalty—a tribute of seven boys and seven girls annually, or in other versions, every nine years, to serve as food for the Minotaur. The number seven is traditionally considered "a sacred, mystical and magical number…symbolizing cosmic and spiritual order and the completion of a natural cycle."[137] Twice seven is fourteen, a number we have seen before with the number of sacrificial parts of the body of Osiris and Dionysos and with the fourteen baskets tended by the

---

[137] J. Tresidder, (Gen. Editor), *The Complete Dictionary of Symbols*, p. 433.

Gerarai in the *Anthesteria* Dionysian festival. Seven boys and seven girls thus are symbolic of a complete tribute of the best—the pure youth (both masculine and feminine) from Athens…a tragic sacrifice.

To return to Ariadne, we see the number of strands that create the fabric of her inherited and childhood *animus*. Her grandfather is Zeus, who came to her grandmother in the form of a White Bull. Her *animus* thus holds a *divine* origin and pure and powerful potential. Her father is a great king, indicating a *noble* aspect to her inner masculine. However, he commits a serious sin of greed against Poseidon, the great god of the sea (the unconscious). As a result, his own wife betrays him in an affair with that which he has kept from the gods (the White Bull), and he must somehow house and feed the fruit of this union, the Minotaur, Ariadne's half-brother.

The Minotaur, this hidden abomination which embodies *primitive, bestial* masculinity, is also a part of Ariadne's *animus*. He lies within the deep recesses of her unconscious as well as her father's, as the labyrinth lies beneath their shared home. Her full brother, Androgeus, was a superb athlete who is murdered out of jealousy. Athleticism is a form of *heroism*. Competitive athletes were rewarded with wreaths in ancient times and with medals in ours, like warriors. Thus we see the heroic strand in her inherited *animus*. Her brother's murder provokes her father to demand the sacrifice of Athenian youth. All of these elements form Ariadne's relationship to the masculine within and outside of herself. She will individuate from her father when Theseus arrives with his fellows for the sacrifice, and through her participation in what follows, her *animus* evolves and achieves ultimately an *Integration,* preparing her for *Individuation.*

Theseus is an Athenian prince who chose, to the dismay of his father, the King of Athens, to go to Crete as one of the sacrificial youths. He went with the intention of slaying the Minotaur. As fate and her psychology would have it, Ariadne falls in love with him. He is "familiar" in that he carries the heroism and nobility native to her *animus* through the imprints of brother and father. He also stands up to the despotism of her father, which offers to liberate her psyche as well as the Athenian youth. This love was the spark of soul needed to free her from the tyranny of unprocessed, primal and destructive masculine energy expressed outwardly by the arrogance and cruelty of her father and embodied by the Minotaur itself. This love activates, as well, her own inner *heroine*. Her *Individuation* requires that she assist in slaying the beast and leave the house and country of her father.

She gives the outer hero, Theseus, a sword along with the clew of thread. The sword will be used to kill this raw, hungry masculine power that tyrannizes all of them, and the thread will help Theseus find his way out of the dark winding unconscious where it dwells. Her gifts to Theseus represent an efficiency both in the weapon she gives him (swords are representative of discernment and discrimination) and in the strategy represented by the thread. She is ready to meet Theseus in the outer world because that heroism was ripe within her own inner *animus*.

He is successful. They sail away towards Athens where she believes she will begin a new life as his wife. But another betrayal is at hand. The ship stops at the island of Naxos and he abandons her there. The story says she falls asleep and wakes to find the ship has sailed. Some versions of the story say she hanged herself.[138] Hanging, swinging (as we saw in the *Anthesteria* celebration), and sleeping all point to a loosening of consciousness. Perhaps too, after the enormous exertion of psychological energy required to rebel against her father and tribal roots, a psychological collapse might be expected to follow. The loosening of consciousness at first engenders an enormous loss and deep heartbreak for Ariadne, but it ultimately brings the arrival of a destiny far greater than she had ever imagined. Dionysos sees her sleeping and falls in love with her. Ultimately, she marries a god, not the human prince, and Dionysos makes her an immortal.

---

[138] Kerényi, *Dionysos*, p. 106.

Jungian analyst and author Ginette Paris writes of her difficulty with this arrival of Dionysos to save Ariadne. Though she comes to interpret it differently, initially it seems to be a story of woman as "victim" seeking and finding yet another savior in a man.[139] What seems to me of special note is that Dionysos is no outer man. He is a *god*, which means he is an archetypal force and an intrapsychic expression. He is also reputed to have been a faithful husband to Ariadne—a unique occurrence in the Greek pantheon. This is quite remarkable and further indicates that what is being portrayed in the myth is the *Integration* and evolution of the masculine *within* Ariadne, to the point that it is an unshakeable, reliable inner support. Her *animus* has fully matured. The cycle of betrayal is finally at an end, and Ariadne experiences the *Coniunctio*—the alchemical "Inner Marriage." Dionysos cherishes her, elevates and supports her internally, and completes her soul in the inner landscape. In the Villa of Mysteries in Pompeii, believed to be a Dionysian initiation chamber, Dionysos is depicted in the frescos of the chamber as resting upon *her* and not the other way around. She is the more encompassing presence. In other words, he becomes a part of *her* larger being, not the reverse.

Plato's romantic idea that each of us comes into this world looking for our other half is intrapsychically correct.[140] Whether or not we find a "soul mate" in the outer world, the most valuable task and highest goal is to develop this marriage within. We become better partners to our outer mates having achieved this and having lifted from them the psychological burden of meeting our projections and needs too large for one human to address for another. There are two interior weddings possible for the human soul: the horizontal union with the *animus/anima* and the vertical union of the soul with the Divine. Each reflects the other at the central axis. Mythically, Ariadne achieves the

---

[139] G. Paris, *Pagan Grace*, p. 41.

[140] Plato, *The Symposium*. Aristophanes' speech. 189d-194e.

intersection of both and this elevates her to triumph over death itself. Dionysos as an archetypal psychic masculine is the "horizontal other," her evolved *animus*. Their union points to the transcendent goal of a vertical wedding of the soul with the Divine. The Bull nature has been humanized and divinized into a beautiful man-god. The primitive masculine represented by the Bull and corrupted into the Minotaur has been transmuted through Ariadne's own courage, transforming into a profoundly supportive and generative sacred inner power.

Now it is time to look at the relationship and distinctions between soul, body, and spirit in regards to the myth and the development of healthy relationship with the contra sexual archetype, the "Other."

8

SOUL, BODY, SPIRIT
DIONYSOS AND CHRIST

Soul and Spirit

Soul and Spirit have become confused in Western consciousness. The distinction began to blur with St. Paul and culminated in the
Council of Constantinople in 869 A.D. It was at this council that human
nature "devolved from a tripartite cosmos of spirit and soul and body
(or matter) to a dualism..."[141] James Hillman elaborates,

> ...the ways of the soul and those of the spirit only
> sometimes coincide... Today we have rather lost this
> difference that most cultures, even tribal ones, know
> and live in terms of. Our distinctions are Cartesian:
> between body and a fuzzy conglomerate of mind,
> psyche and spirit. We have lost the third, middle
> position...the threefold division has collapsed into two
> because soul had become identified with spirit.[142]

Hillman identifies this event as a loss in clarification of the
nuances of soul. Rudolf Steiner (1861-1925), Austrian philosopher,
social reformer, and esotericist, was even more impressed with the
effects of this Church Council. He stressed the loss of a personal

---

[141] J. Hillman, *Peaks and Vales,* in J. Hillman (Ed.), *Puer Papers*, p. 54.
[142] J. Hillman, *Re-Visioning Psychology*, p. 67, 68.

connection with Spirit, leaving that domain to sacerdotal authority.[143] From either perspective, by collapsing Soul and Spirit, Western culture has lost a vital ingredient in understanding humanity.

Soul and Body

Dionysos is connected with Soul and it is Soul that is deeply connected to Body. In the tradition of depth psychology, it is in the deep and in the dark that we truly touch soul. It is through passion (*pathos)* that we experience the intensity of our being and engage in "soul-making."

> Soul-making then involves particularly the deepening qualities of those moments when we fall apart, only to be renewed. These are the pathologizing motions of the soul, our *pathos,* or suffering, necessary to a contact with mystery... This is a falling deep into the dark of the west, where the sun sets into the sea.[144]

It is here that we meet the suffering, passionate god Dionysos.

> In Greek thought soul and body were generally in-divisible.[145]

The Body and its instincts were considered the medium of the Soul.

> Instinctual nature is not only the vehicle for biological processes but it also conveys the emotional feeling tones of life in a way that could well be described as the language of the soul.[146]

---

[143] R. Steiner, *Freedom and the Catholic Church*, Lecture III of III, Dornach, June 6, 1920.

[144] Hillman, Re-Visioning Psychology, p. 53.

[145] J. Hillman, *The Myth of Analysis*, p. 207.

[146] N. Qualls-Corbett, *The Sacred Prostitute*, p. 86.

Through the Body, the Soul talks. Soul speaks through our desires and fears, in the ecstasy or dysfunction of sexual union, in the distress of disease, and even in simple aches and pains.

> If Dionysos is the Lord of Souls, he is the soul of nature, its psychic interiority. His "dismemberment" is the fragments of consciousness strewn through all of life, through every erogenous zone and plexus of our physical bodies.[147]

When we cultivate reverent attention to the Body—both our own and that body of our mother, the earth—we are communing at the same time with Soul. To commune with Soul, we need to become lovingly present to Body, our own and hers.

Sex and the Divine, The Goat and the Lamb

The Pauline-based Christian view has likewise perpetrated a schism between Body/Soul, and the Holy, leading to a deep sense of alienation. The goat, already associated with sin in the Jewish tradition, became emblematic of troublesome bodily instinct, especially male sexuality.[148]

The goat was a sacred totem of Dionysos, while the lamb has been associated with Jesus. While the goat is emblematic of instinct and individuality, the lamb represents purity, docility, and community. Sheep are found in herds and easily follow, while goats go their own way. For two millennia, the difference between goat and lamb has been emphasized, with the lamb being worshipped, and the goat demonized.

Anti-goat consciousness began with the Judaism of Biblical times. The idea of the "scapegoat" came from the Jewish custom of

---

[147] Hillman, *The Myth of Analysis*, p. 280.
[148] Herder Lexikon, *The Herder Symbol Dictionary*, p. 87.

heaping the sins of the people upon a literal goat and driving it into the wilderness on the yearly Day of Atonement, Yom Kippur. The dietary laws of Kashrut (keeping "kosher") are based on the injunction from Exodus 23:19, Exodus 34:26, and Deuteronomy 14:21, all stating, "You shall not boil a kid in its mother's milk." This was precisely the ritual practiced in Dionysian sacrificial rites. It would seem the Semetic people were adamant to create a distinction between their worship and that of their neighbors who followed Dionysos.[149]
Many Biblical references speak of separating lambs from goats.

> We have translated this in our modern Western minds as separating the right from the wrong, the noble from the ignoble, the righteous from the unrighteous. That mythology has been built into us so deeply that the goat quality, the ecstatic Dionysian quality, still does not function in us today.[150]

The goat ultimately became symbolic of evil.

> "Dionysus Melangius," Dionysus of the Black Goatskin, was an ancient scapegoat-satyr form of the god, whose appearance greatly influenced the medieval Christian notion of what the devil should look like. To this day, the devil is pictured with the goat's horns, cloven hooves, and tail. In medieval Christian Europe, goats were renowned for their lechery and were said to be familiars of witches.[151]

---

[149] C. Kerenyi, *Dionysos*, p. 254-255.
[150] R. Johnson, *Ecstasy*, p. 45.
[151] Johnson, *Ecstasy*, p. 46.

The Goat and the Witch

Indeed, the goat as the Dionysian principle is the primordial companion of the dark "witch" feminine. Jungian analyst J. Marvin Spiegelman sees the dark feminine or "witch" archetype as the natural complement of the sexual masculine. She is a *feminine Logos* to his *masculine Eros*.

> The archetype of the witch is also bringing a new form of consciousness—a new logos… This new form of consciousness is quite different from that having prevailed for many hundreds of years. It is personal rather than impersonal, concrete rather than abstract, individual rather than collective, magical rather than scientific, irrational rather than rational.[152]

The "witch" archetype is analogous to the Biblical Lilith, she of the dark or black moon, with her witchy power to seduce and destroy.

A healing, however, perpetrated by psyche through dreams and fantasies appears to have been taking place. In 1970, Spiegelman was already noting the trend in the material his clients were bringing to the consulting room. Here are images that merged sexuality and divinity. In the article "Notes from the Underground" published in the 1970 issue of *Spring Magazine,* he writes,

> …the new shocking thing for our western consciousness is the re-divinization of sexuality. That God can have a penis *as well as* all-seeing eye! That God can make love, *as well as* preach about it! I think these are hints of the new god-image. He is a demon, and from the Underworld, but he is not the devil, nor even *a* devil. The devil of Christian tradition is an unavoidable

---

[152] J.M. Spiegelman, "Notes from the Underground," *Spring Magazine*, p. 209-210.

negative brother to the all-positive Jesus-image of God. The emerging image is different. He is demonic as passion and love and sexuality can be demonic…This demon is no devil; he simply includes those aspects of love previously rejected by the conscious acceptance of love as purely *Agape*.[153]

What has occurred in the interim, nearly fifty years later? A plethora of material and speculation about Mary Magdalene's relationship with Jesus has inundated the media, the publication of *The Sexuality of Christ in Renaissance Art and Modern Oblivion* by Leo Sternberg in 1983, the same year that *Holy Blood and Holy Grail* was published, and the publication of Dan Brown's mega-popular novel, *The Da Vinci Code,* which was subsequently made into a motion picture grossing $758.2 million, released in 2006.

At the time of this writing, a television show based on the DC Marvel Comics character, *Lucifer*, has just been given a second season after its initial 13 episodes. The Dionysian is overt in this depiction of Lucifer. His accomplice is a dark, intriguing and deeply loyal female *lilim*—or daughter of Lilith. Their earthly home is a bar/nightclub in Los Angeles, called Lux (meaning light). Bars, of course, resonate with the Dionysian theme. The story follows the development of empathy and compassion—virtues of relatedness—in a figure heretofore notoriously associated with evil. He is far more Dionysian in depiction than cold Satanic evil.

Meanwhile, on the more academic front, the classical Greek Platonic term *Anima Mundi* (Soul of the World), has gained currency. An interest in the "Sophia" of nature, and, as discussed earlier, the Dark Madonna images of the holy feminine have captured popular imagination. Environmental concerns flood the media. Systems theory, which views reality as syncretic systems rather than discrete parts,

---

[153] Spiegelman, "Notes from the Underground," *Spring Magazine*, p. 204.

permeates all of the sciences from physics to cultural anthropology. More mundane, yet practically valuable, efforts of composting and recycling are entering common practice in our cities, illustrating a growing care for the environment—Earth's body. "Mindfulness" and "somatic awareness" pervade psychotherapy and the healing arts. And the understanding of gender is in massive change.

This is by no means a comprehensive list. But it is enough to indicate a profoundly significant change in the zeitgeist. I suspect that this list will continue to grow. It would appear that, albeit at times quite clumsily, and often in a far too literal manner (hidden, yet in plain sight) the Spiritual Christ is integrating Dionysian Soul while the feminine is being resacralized in recovered reverence for the Earth and the human body.

More about Christ and Dionysos

As we have seen with Dionysos, Jesus was known to have had female friends and followers. He talked with women and, contrary to the milieu, he did not judge them as inferior. He protected women, as evinced by his defense of the woman who was about to be stoned for adultery,[154] and of the woman who anointed Him,[155] as well as the bleeding woman who touched His garment (blood is considered a defilement in traditional Judaism).[156] His first miracle was at the bequest of His mother.[157] The very fact that it was Mary Magdalene who was reported to have first encountered Him after the resurrection illustrates the extraordinary significance given to women in His

---

[154] John 8; 1-11.

[155] Luke 7: 36-37.

[156] Matthew 9:20.

[157] John 2:1-11.

ministry.[158] Clearly, Jesus did not discriminate against women. He was neither sexist nor racist according to the accounts. He neither patronized nor condemned. He was born in lowly circumstance and mostly travelled on the road in a simple fashion. He was not urban or materialistically privileged. Reminiscent of Dionysos, he said,

> "I am the true vine, and my Father is the vine grower. He removes every branch in me that bears no fruit. Every branch that bears fruit he prunes to make it bear more fruit."[159]

The list goes on:

> Jesus and Dionysus are both sons of divine fathers and mortal, virgin mothers. Christ harrowed Hell, Dionysus emerged from the underworld... At Eleusis the followers of Dionysus celebrated his "Advent" with a newborn baby placed in a winnowing basket—the forerunner of baby Jesus in a manger. Both Jesus and Dionysus die...are reborn, symbolizing the life that does not end...And of course, the wine. One of Jesus' miracles was turning water into wine, something Dionysus can be said to do on a regular basis... Eucharist is a ceremony of *ex stasis*, drinking the wine, the blood of God, and transcending time and space to become for a moment divine.[160]

Both Dionysos and Christ share the values of Liberty and Equality. Unlike the societies in which their stories are told, they promote unity and spurn elitism. They are not constricted by

[158] Mark 16: 9, Luke 24:10.

[159] John 15:1-2

[160] R. Johnson, *Ecstasy*, p. 31-32.

socialization and demand that their followers also risk thinking for themselves. Jesus' words, "If anyone comes to Me and does not hate father and mother, wife and children, brothers and sisters, yes, and even life itself, he/she cannot be my disciple,"[161] might just as easily been spoken by Dionysos if "life" here is meant to be taken as the false life of the personality bound by social mores and "father and mother, etc." as those prejudices and sanctions handed down through tribe. Jesus and Dionysos both emphasize honesty in one's relationship with Spirit and find hypocrisy reprehensible.

How does Christ differ from Dionysos? Every effort seems to have been made to uplift Christ and demonize Dionysos. But what if Christ is the evolution of the Dionysian? What if Christ is an *Integration* and evolution of Jerusalem and Athens? Or, perhaps Dionysos is a *soul* expression of the higher *Spiritual* frequency of Christ? What if both are held in companionship in our consciousness? The significant difference between them, I have concluded, is the compassion of Christ. Dionysos is certainly ruthless when slighted, whereas Jesus, as Christ, advises "turn the other cheek."[162] Jesus demonstrates *wisdom* and because of that wisdom, His love is patient and all-embracing. Dionysos more easily exercises revenge. Thus, I conclude that Dionysos relates to the soul of woman as a rich *psychological* support—more of a "soul mate" on the *horizontal* plane of life—while the Christ is on the *vertical* axis as *Spiritual* goal.

However, in this study, I am hoping to highlight the need and indeed the current process of a rapprochement between the two. Jesus clearly demonstrates many positive Dionysian characteristics. In fact, when he chases out the money changers from "His Father's house,"[163] he is acting in passionate retributive Dionysian fashion. Neither Jesus

---

[161] Luke 14:26.

[162] Matthew 5:39.

[163] Matthew 21:12.

nor Dionysos are tolerant of irreverence. This is a weighty realization. We live in highly irreverent times and neither Jesus nor Dionysos has tolerance for an irreverent humanity.[164] Contemporary children are no longer taught reverence, and they have no examples of reverence. Parents do not demonstrate reverence for their own souls, nor show reverence towards any significant ideals. Most don't exhibit reverence towards one another or their children. In an irreverent world, the Earth herself falls victim. If reverence *is* present, it is highly misplaced, as in reverence for those who have amassed great wealth and for entertainment and athletic "stars." If we are to truly follow Christ or Dionysos, reverence for what is truly important, for *life*, must once again be cultivated.

The Church, meaning all denominations of Christianity, has defended itself against anything "pagan" for the past two thousand years. This was understandable in the early formation of the Christian paradigm and spreading its message. But now that Christianity has succeeded in penetrating every corner of the world and all cultures, might Christianity be less defensive and reclaim that which would only enrich Christian religion, philosophy and psychology? The Dionysian appreciation and celebration of holy matter/mother/earth/and the feminine might even save us from destroying this beautiful planet home upon which we depend.

Dionysos and Symbols of Enlightenment

Dionysos was said to be reborn at the Winter Solstice in the Korykian or Corycian Cave high on the slopes of Mount Parnassus. The sun, humanity's foremost symbol of enlightenment, literally lighting our world, begins again its half-year ascendancy, bringing

---

[164] The requirement of reverence in considering the archetype of Dionysos was pointed out to me by Judah Pollack after attending a reading of the Bacchae presented by Paul Woodruff at the C.G. Jung Institute, San Francisco, April 9, 2016.

increase of light after the darkest and shortest day of the year. Jesus' birth is celebrated at this same time because, in the Northern Hemisphere, the archetypal resonance is appropriate. Jesus is *the* light-bringer for Christianity. In reference to the discussion regarding goat and lamb, Jesus' birth, like Dionysos', is celebrated during the month attributed to the sign of the goat, Capricorn. Jesus, in his direct relationship with God, exemplifies the path of the mystic, while Dionysos is he of "mystic madness."[165] Mystics, like goats, are mountain climbers and individualists seeking ever-greater proximity to the light.

Like Jesus, Dionysos is born in a cave. Caves represent first and foremost the womb of the mother, matter. Dionysos' birth is specifically said to have occurred in an *elevated* cave. I believe this unique detail in Dionysos' myth has significance. The rebirth of Dionysos takes place in a cave on a holy mountain. Mountains are quintessentially symbolic of "the heights," i.e., transcendence. Holy Mountains are found worldwide. The alchemical image of the "Mountain of the Philo-sophers," the *Abiegnus* (literally "fir-covered mountain," reminiscent of Dionysos and his association with the pine), symbolizes Initiation and the journey towards achieving the spiritual treasure.[166] Jesus' Trans-figuration into a body of light was witnessed by three of His apostles on Mount Tabor.[167]

An analogy with scaling the heights can be made with the human body. Located deep, but **elevated within** the brain, is an endocrine gland, the pineal, also described as a *"cave"* which senses light and is responsible for the production of melatonin and serotonin, chemicals which regulate sleep and mood. Dimethyltryptamine (DMT), produced by the pineal gland, is believed to play a role in altered and mystical states of consciousness. DMT is also found in

---

[165] D. Fideler, *Restoring the Soul of the World*, p. 40.

[166] J. Wasserman, *The Mystery Traditions, Secret Symbols and Art*, p. 50.

[167] Matthew 17:1-13.

psychedelic plant substances including peyote, ayahuasca, and mushrooms further stimulating the pineal gland by ingestion. Dionysos is the god of altered states of consciousness, thus the correlation is consistent.

The pineal gland is called the Third Eye in the chakra teachings of the East and is literally and symbolically associated with light. In its synthesis and secretion of melatonin, information is communicated about visible light streaming from the environment towards the body. The Third Eye has a real relationship with light and apparently, too, with more subtle forms of light, i.e., "enlightenment."

The Thyrsus and Kundalini

Another interesting analogue is the name of the gland itself. The pineal gland is named for its pinecone shape; and the staff attributed specifically to Dionysos is topped with a pinecone. Dionysos' *thyrsus* staff is traditionally made from a fennel stalk and depicted with ivy entwining it. Fennel has an interesting history in Greek myth. When Prometheus stole fire from the gods for the benefit of mankind, he hid it in a fennel stalk.[168] Thus divine fire, the holy fire, which enlivens, is associated with the stalk, which is integral to his sacred staff.

Dionysos' *thyrsus* resembles Hermes' staff, the caduceus, a present-day emblem of the medical profession. A well-known Kundalini symbol in the East, the caduceus represents the spinal column and the entwining snakes signify the energies that run up the spine. The *thyrsus* is entwined with ivy. Ivy and snakes appear to have been interchangeable symbols, as Dionysos' devotees were reported to have worn *either* snake or ivy wreaths. Thus Dionysos' staff might also be seen as representative of the fiery Kundalini and the spinal column.

---

[168] Larousse, *World Mythology*, Prometheus, p. 112.

The goal of the Kundalini force is literally the pineal gland and its subtle counterpart, the Third Eye or Sixth Chakra. It is in the Pineal that enlightenment is said to take place...the golden light illuminates the cave. The mind/consciousness experiences enlightenment. Basically, the symbols of the caduceus and the *thyrsus* are the same. Early on, we saw that Shiva and Dionysos are believed to have had definite archetypal affinity, so it is not surprising that associated symbolism would find translation from East to West. Whether the symbol traveled from East to West or if it is an archetype realized by both cultures, the same experiences are expressed.

According to Plato,[169] there are four types of divine madness or *mania* sent by the gods, they are:

> ...not to be confused with insanity—that took the soul outside of itself to experience a larger reality. Poetic madness was sent by the Muses. Mystic madness was sent by Dionysus, the god of ecstasy and liberation. Prophetic madness was sent by far-seeing Apollo. And erotic madness was sent by Aphrodite, the goddess of love.[170]

The path of mysticism is always seeking communion and sometimes, with a total dissolution of a sense of separation, union, with the Divine. The goal is this experience, and the results are the spiritualization of the physical, the ordinary, the matter of everyday life. *Enlightenment* is another name for the aim of this divine madness. The density of matter and life, as it is experienced, is infused with life-giving Spirit.

---

[169] Plato, *Phaedrus,* 265B.

[170] D. Fideler, *Restoring the Soul of the World,* p. 40.

9

THE "CHEMICAL WEDDING" OF ARIADNE AND DIONYSOS

Alchemy, Initiation and Individuation

Alchemy emerged when no division existed between science and everyday life, or the sacred and spiritual. To apply spiritual intention to the physical was understood to effect subtler levels. The division we experience in the modern Western world was not the way in which our predecessors viewed life. This gradual movement towards differentiation in the West is well summed up by Jung:

> Western man is held in thrall by the "the ten thousand things"; he sees only particulars, he is ego-bound and thing-bound, and unaware of the deep root of all being. Eastern man, on the other hand, experiences the world of particulars, and even his own ego, like a dream; he is rooted essentially in the "Ground," which attracts him so powerfully that his relations with the world are relativized to a degree that is often incomprehensible to us.[171]

East and West have polarized, but when Alchemy took hold of the Western imagination, we were not yet so utterly enthralled by "the ten thousand things." Alchemy is thought to have its roots in ancient Egypt, India and Tibet, and China, and entered into Europe with the occupation of the Moors (711-1492 AD), who invaded Spain from

---

[171] Jung, *Psychology and Alchemy,* p. 7-8, CW 12, ¶ 8.

North Africa.[172] The Western alchemical paradigm is very much related to the Hermetic tradition, which takes as a foundational premise, "As Above, So Below."[173] In other words, life is holographic. What is accomplished here has its reflection on the spiritual level, and *vice versa*.

Alchemy is interested in resolving the opposition of polarities, of "infusing matter with spirit and rendering spirit material, of the necessity of purifying the practitioner's nature, so that his or her substance could be purified, and *vice versa*."[174] The goal is described in physical terms as "gold," and in spiritual terms, as attaining "The Lapis," "the Philosopher's Stone," or "The Elixir," which is believed to ensure eternal life, elevate the soul, and wed it to the spirit. These are all metaphors for achieving enlightenment.

> The Stone is the arcanum of all arcana, possessing the power to perfect imperfection in all things…it is the figure of light veiled in dark matter, that divine love essence which combines divine wisdom and creative power, often identified with Christ as creative Logos, or with the Eastern idea of the *atman* symbolized by the jewel in the lotus.[175]

The investigations of alchemy led to present-day chemistry, which is now entirely divorced from its original spiritual *raison d'être*. Apparently, there were materialists even in that earlier époque, whom the more authentic alchemists referred to as "puffers," those who literalized the goal of the work, being concerned only with physical results, i.e., gold-making. But true alchemists undertook their own refinement even as they were perfecting the minerals in their laboratories. They were devoted and humble, as evinced by woodcuts

---

[172] A. Aromatico, *Alchemy: The Great Secret,* p. 14.

[173] The Emerald Tablet.

[174] Aromatico, *Alchemy: The Great Secret,* p. 15.

[175] L. Abraham, *A Dictionary of Alchemical Imagery,* p. 145.

depicting them at prayer in their laboratories; and they recognized that the work was always finished by grace, not by their own will.[176]

From the alchemical point of view, everything is related, from the densest of matter to the most subtle expressions of soul and spirit. Minerals have their counterparts in the six traditional planets and the Sun. So the alchemist worked to refine every derivative—every metal—to its purest state, the solar gold, which is unable to tarnish. They envisioned gold as the Sun's pure presence in the mineral world.

The planets and metals likewise found their counterparts in the subtle body system of the chakras. Each chakra is related to a metal and to its corresponding planet. The Sun=gold rests in and emanates from the heart chakra, and its *mental* realization is located in Mercury=quicksilver quality of the mind, found in the pineal-gland chakra. Mercury, literally being the closest planet to the radiant Sun, bespeaks this close affinity. As we have discovered, Dionysos' *thyrsus* takes us right up to the pineal gland with its theme of enlightenment and mystic state of consciousness. An honorable alchemist was a mystic who strove to do a holy work to the best of her or his ability. The alchemist was a *theurgist*—a "god worker"—working on behalf of the Divine to perfect nature—around, and also within, himself. There were women as well as men alchemists. One of the most famous was Maria Prophetissa, otherwise known as Mary, the Jewess, or Miriam, the Prophetess. She was reputed to have lived between the first and third centuries, A.D.[177]

Alchemy involves a series of stages that lead to *mortificatio*, death, and ultimately regeneration at a higher level, commonly symbolized by *the chemical wedding*, (the alchemical wedding). It was understood that the great dilemma lay in the antagonism of opposites we experience in life, which has its ultimate expression in alienation from the divine source. The *chemical wedding*, the uniting of opposites

---

[176] Heinrich Khunrath, *Amphitheatrum sapientiae aeternae, 1602,* and the plates in the *Mutus Liber*, published in 1677.

[177] M. Haeffner, *The Dictionary of Alchemy,* p. 169.

into a harmonious union, was the goal. It was achieved through repeated cycles of dissolution and coagulation, dissolving and reconstituting, with ever-more-refined results. A psychological death, what we would describe in modern terms as dissolution of ego-defense constructs, was a necessary element in the process. The alchemist did the work, but it was understood that grace or the Divine, in the end, finished it. The alchemist put in the effort with reverence and devotion, but he was not in danger of inflation, having the understanding that it was ultimately by grace that success was possible. The diminishment of the ego of the alchemist was, in fact, essential to the process.

It was through the marriage of opposites that something new and enduring emerged, symbolized by the Stone, the Elixir, or Gold. Carl Jung spent the last twenty years of his life ardently studying the imagery of alchemy, convinced that it illustrated the labor of the human soul in its efforts to evolve to a higher state. In our study, the marriage of Dionysos and Ariadne might be understood as that goal, *the chemical wedding*, emblematic of the alchemical achievement of refinement, confirmed by Ariadne's new name, "Aridela," "The Clear (or Shining) One." She has successfully achieved the Lapis, the Philosopher's Stone, within her own consciousness.

The Chemical (Alchemical) Wedding

Ariadne and the goddess Persephone are archetypally related in their familiarity with the Underworld, the dark depths of the human psyche. However, Ariadne does not make a *return* trip each year from earth to the depths, but through her wedding to Dionysos is elevated to a spiritual, cosmic level, becoming "Aridela," *the clear or shining one*. She is "refined" to transparency, having died and been reborn. While Persephone is married to the Lord of the Underworld and fated to return each year, Ariadne is married to the Lord of *Zoë*, that is, of life, death, and transmutation (grapes into wine) and achieves the alchemical goal sought by the alchemists: true happiness and eternal life.

The archetype of the success of the alchemical work was the *androgyne*, the balanced co-mingling of opposites. As we have seen, Ariadne's own *animus* is activated positively, while Dionysos himself, blends the features of both sexes, along with being in positive relationship to the Earth Mother and the feminine. Each thus represents a balance of masculine and feminine *within themselves* and together they form *two wholes in harmonious union*, rather than two incomplete halves to one whole. Ariadne, a whole, rather than half, psychologically illustrates the Jungian goal of *Individuation*.

Wine, Dionysos' special elixir, is the quintessential alchemical substance. The process of *fermentation* literally inspirits the juice of the grape. "The juice of grapes or wine is the *aqua permanens* or mercurial water, also known as the alchemist's secret fire."[178] The use of wine liturgically in Christianity is understood, at least on an unconscious level, to make perfect sense. Not only does imbibing it literally warm and lift one's spirit, but the art and craft of wine-making is itself alchemical.

Ultimately, the alchemist's goal is the alchemy of the *Self*—the alchemist should become inspirited. When one drinks the consecrated wine, from an alchemical view, one is seeking to commune with the Divine and to elevate one's soul to the level of spirit. When one eats the consecrated bread — also a product of alchemy by virtue of fermentation — the body, represented by the wafer, is sanctified. The ultimate goal would be to evolve oneself: to be, as Christ exemplified, a perfected nexus of Spirit and Matter. The wine represents the god, while the bread represents the Earth Mother whose totem was always sheaves of wheat.[179] Here again we see the pattern of the masculine life force in partnership with the holy "mater"/matter, as we know it in Dionysos' relationship with the Earth Mother.

Initiation in the ancient mystery schools was likewise a spiritual alchemy, with rapprochement to the god as its goal. Whereas the

---

[178] L. Abraham, *A Dictionary of Alchemical Imagery*, p. 90.

[179] B. G. Walker, *The Woman's Dictionary of Symbols and Sacred Objects*, p. 482.

Maenads seemed to have simply surrendered to and been possessed by spirit at an instinctual level, the later Dionysian Orphic rites appear to have had a more conscious soul work approach. In special rites, the neophyte had a life-changing experience that was calculated to transform her into an Initiate, someone who had seen truth hidden to the profane, and would begin to live life in a whole new way, from a new state of consciousness. "The general Greek word for "rite" comes from a root meaning "grow up," and that is exactly what a rite is: a ceremony for growing up."[180]

Carl Jung's enormous contribution was to bring back the mysteries and reframe their language in psychological terms, liberating the message from the bonds of organized religions. He made recognition of the soul and the "work" of human spiritual evolution available to the individual outside of doctrinal affiliation. The evolution of a woman's soul has particular affinity to the Dionysian mysteries or ancient and classical times. Archetypal patterns do not die, they simply take on new forms. For two thousand years, Western women have been bereft of instruction specifically fitting feminine psychology.

In 1909, a marvelous *temenos* (sacred space) was uncovered, a Villa containing an intriguing chamber whose walls depicted a decidedly Dionysian sequence of events, pointing to the strong possibility that this place had been the site of women's Dionysian initiation rites. The house is located on the outskirts of the small town of Pompeii, just south of Naples, which had lay buried since the fateful and terrible eruption of Mount Vesuvius in 79 AD. The chamber contains ten images, evocative of the classic alchemical treatises: *The Rosarium Philosophorum* and the *Splendor Solis*, as well as the Zen Buddhist Ten Oxherding pictures that depict the purification of the mind and the progress of Enlightenment. It is here that Roman females are believed to have experienced a spiritual wedding exclusively meant to empower and fulfill them as women.

---

[180] K. Bradway, *Villa of Mysteries*, p. 1.

10

INITIATION AND INDIVIDUATION
THE WOMEN OF POMPEII AND THE WOMEN OF TODAY

It is nearly dusk on an early June evening. The cobblestone road that leads through Porta Ercolano, one of the city gates that leads out of the ancient city of Pompeii, is deserted. On either side, millennia old sarcophagi of a necropolis stand sentinel. This is my first day in Pompeii, and I am on my way to the goal of the journey, "The Villa of Mysteries," uncovered in 1909, after nearly 2000 years of resting hidden under thirty feet of volcanic ash and soil deposited by the sudden, devastating eruption of Mount Vesuvius in 79 A.D.

That violent eruption, the first in 700 years, buried the entire city and environs within three days. The explosion ultimately released a hundred thousand times the thermal energy released by the Hiroshima bombing in World War II.[181] At least 1000 souls perished, and it irrevocably destroyed the lives of every inhabitant. That horrific tragedy paradoxically turned out to be extreme good fortune for history. Architecture, art, human and animal remains, and even foodstuffs were wonderfully preserved, allowing accurate re-construction of the life lived by Roman citizens during the classical period.

As I walk with slow intention towards the Villa, I imagine what it might have been like for a woman to be approaching the Villa two

---

[181] "Science: *Man of Pompeii." Time*, Oct. 15, 1956.

millennia ago in anticipation of her initiation. It is not difficult to relate to her. Like contemporary Western women, free women of the Roman Empire were exposed to learning and culture, yet they also lived in a patriarchal culture that increasingly devalued the feminine. I sense I am approaching a sacred place, a space from which I, too, will emerge a changed woman. Nothing will be the same for the woman I am imagining 2000 years ago, and also for myself, today. I walk carefully with presence and sacred intention in expectation of what will be revealed. Like those women—though I know something of the mythology of their religion—I do not know what to expect in the chamber. I hope I am able to hear and see clearly, or at least get a hint of what is there, whispering through the walls and floor, through the images, through the presence of the sacred in that space. I hope, in some small way, to understand their story and how it relates to myself and my sisters today.

The Villa itself was at least 200 years old at the time of the 79 A.D. eruption and had undergone expansion several times. Archaeological excavation has revealed a building of about 40,000 square feet with at least sixty rooms. It is believed that the Villa hosted guests but also provided living space for priestesses and adherents to the mystery religion of Dionysos when it was used for that purpose. The room which is of particular interest in our study is what archaeologists mostly agree had been an Orphic Dionysian Initiation Chamber.[182] It is 7 x 5 meters (23 x 16 ft.) and is found around the corner from the *exedra*, or curved patio, at the center of one side of the Villa.

This room is believed to have been used as an Initiation Chamber for women into the Dionysian mysteries from 31 BC-14 AD. It is also believed that this ritual was specifically for *mature* women, as evinced in the frescoes. Not only are women prevalent in the murals

---

[182] A. Maiuri, *Villa Dei Misteri*, p. 81.

but there are also wedding rings on the left hands of several of the figures, as well as clothing which specifically indicate the status of married women, not young girls. Girls married as young teens at the time. The women depicted are not adolescents. The colors of the clothing indicate that these were women who came from educated strata of society. The saffron and Tyrian purple dyes could be afforded only by women of means who, like women of today, could inherit property and own businesses. Free Pompeiian women had a good many legal rights and standing within their society.

The room itself depicts a magnificent drama of breathtaking beauty encircling the space. While the frescoes are divided into ten panels, figures move across their boundaries, indicating a clockwise fluid movement that culminates with figures depicting peaceful balance and a resolution to the preceding action. Because it is believed that this chamber was the site of the ritual of Dionysian initiation, it is perhaps best to begin with an explanation of ritual and initiation.

Ritual and Initiation

Ritual, in its highest intention, understood from a Jungian perspective, is the activation of powerful latent energy in the un-conscious through the orchestrated use of archetypal symbols, including images, scents, and sounds. Archetypal symbols are, from this point of view, our "mother tongue," predating acquisition of language and transcending time and culture. The psyche, on deeper levels than the conscious mind, speaks to us every night in this symbolic multilayered language in the form of dreams. A good ritual is constructed specifically to trigger a response not only in conscious perception but in the greater psyche as well, through the use of this language. The intention of ritual would be to heal and/or enrich the participant.

A ritual should take you into a much broader, richer experience; every time you go through a ritual you should contact that deepest, divine part of yourself and open to something new.[183]

An *initiation* ritual would do what the word "initiation" describes. It would *initiate,* begin, a process of transformation leading to psychological and spiritual healing and growth in the participant. The inner experience sparked by such a ceremony can entirely shift one's orientation to life and give added depth to one's character. It is believed that the Villa provided this opportunity *to* women, *by* women, who were drawn to the path of Ariadne and Dionysos. Jungian analyst M. Esther Harding writes,

> The reality of the main figures (Ariadne and Dionysos in the center panel)[184] makes it clear that the series is not merely the representation of a myth, but is rather intended to portray the inner psychological reality of certain mythic happenings, as they might be re-presented by one undergoing a profound psychological experience in which the background material and drama, which are usually entirely unconscious, are activated.[185]

Experiencing the Initiation Chamber

Though no one can definitively interpret the meaning of the images, their evocative depiction of Orphic Dionysian themes encourages conjecture with some sense of approximate accuracy. The

[183] M. Woodman, *Conscious Femininity*, p. 32.

[184] Parenthesis mine.

[185] M.E. Harding, *Dreaming in Red*, Introduction, p. 6.

panels convey archetypal information, i.e., symbolism with worldwide meaning, as well as those with specifically Dionysian/Orphic content. Thus, though no written authorization as to their meaning survives, we can venture an educated guess.

A key to understanding the images is not simply having our ideas *about* them, but *experiencing* them directly in the room. This was the foremost objective and my only real justification for the 6300-mile journey to enter the chamber. There is a fine line between experience and the naming of that experience, in the quest for intimacy we seek. Information can deepen understanding, but experience gives a *felt* knowing. Though I entered the room with some knowledge, I worked to push it aside to simply *be with* the images. I will begin with that, and hope to weave in the ideas that may create meaning for you, my reader.

As I look from panel to panel, a full range of experiences unfolds.[186] Beauty, *extraordinary* beauty:... colors of richness and depth like the visceral blood rich red background and ladies dressed in citrine/topaz and amethyst, and accents of emerald (all jewel tones); a solemnity; pastoral peace and sweetness... followed by terror and intimations of madness and enlightenment; the promise of wholeness and completion; holy awe; intense surrender, vulnerability and sub-mission; suffering, intense suffering followed by a sweet joy and transcendence and ultimately an Integration in a new balance, feeling the approval of the gods; joy, peace, equilibrium, wholeness. All this, supported by a black-and-white floor, configuring the opposites in its complementary tiles. These were the emotions and the sense of unfolding as I walked the sacred space of this mandala of images. Jungian analyst Nor Hall's description of the red backdrop of the panels speaks closely to my experience:

> The red of Dionysus belongs to women. So dark it is almost black, it calls up old wine, deep wounds, and the

---

[186] Please review the images of the frescoes at the back of the book.

marbled walls of the womb itself, heavy with twisted veins reaching inevitably toward the heart. At the heart of the mystery chamber...in Pompeii there is an un-abashed love of women. Especially experienced women like the *Domina,* who sits at the far end of the room as if at the far end of our book's trajectory, welcoming newcomers to her *thiasos*: the company of women who "have been through it" and survived.[187]

The theme of intensity, the extreme range of feeling available to the human heart, a clear indication of the presence of the Dionysian, is undeniable.

We will soon explore the panels in detail, but a review of general impressions might serve to appreciate the gestalt of the series. The theme of opposites is strikingly apparent throughout.

The heavily clothed and veiled woman at the start is succeeded by women in less formal attire. Further along in the series, a naked, yet draped, woman bends over the knees of another woman. Then even the drape gives way to the rearview of the fully and exquisitely lovely nude dancer in the eighth panel.

A quiet scene of women making preparations in the dress of their time and culture, in the preliminary scenes, gives way to an entirely mythical and pastoral scene quite outside urban concerns.

Some figures wear shoes, others are barefoot. The central figures of Dionysos and Ariadne each wear one shoe, while the other foot is bare, surely a significant detail.

Urbane meets pastoral, and "the liminal," that place between two worlds, is the underlying rhythm. The sweet pastoral scene portraying mythical figures of Silenus, who looks suspiciously like

---

[187] N. Hall, *Dreaming in Red*, Preface, p. V.

Socrates, the embodiment of wisdom at that time, is accompanied by a panisk, fauns, and kids at play.[188]

This gentle pastoral scene is immediately followed by the "terrified woman" who is turning away and seeming to flee from a subsequent scene that inspires great dread. What has appeared all sweetness has now turned to terror.

Following the centrally placed oversized figure of Dionysos reclining languorously on a seated feminine figure wearing a wedding ring and thought to be his bride, Ariadne, we come to a shockingly powerful determined dark-winged angel preparing to strike the bare back of a woman who rests her head in the lap of another.

That scene is immediately followed by a beautiful nude woman who seems to have the same features as the prostrate woman, now dancing and playing cymbals held high above her head.

The tableau concludes with a woman who seems to be the same as the previous figures, preparing to return to the world, her hair being coifed by another woman while an *erote* (a Cupid figure) holds up a mirror. From the adjoining wall, another *erote* looks on holding a bow, but no arrow.

The whole movement replete with contrasting moods and images concludes with what has been called the *Domina*, seated comfortably, looking towards the central figures of Ariadne and Dionysos, from whence the round begins again.

The Meaning

Linda Fierz-David has done an admirable job in analyzing the images from a Jungian, depth-archetypal perspective. However, all we have is the visuals and thus no definitive interpretations. Any interpretation is surely slanted by the writer's perspective, experience

---

[188] L. Fierz-David, *Dreaming in Red*, p. 59; Plato, *Symposium*, (trans.) Francis Birrell and Shane Leslie, p. 88.

and training. I can only write from my own experience of the room, bringing to bear what is known about Orphism and also archetypal psychology.

The experience of being in the chamber itself is very much like being in a dream. There is a sea of evocative images, many of which are archetypal and deeply symbolic, inviting us to go deeper. As such, the experience is not only significant from the point of view of the collective psyche, but also powerfully invites the viewer to her own personal experience.

But in a most general purview, all the realistically drawn figures in the unfolding story are women, except for the young boy child at the start who looks at a scroll. Only the mythological scenes depict the masculine. This strongly indicates that what is depicted has to do specifically with women and with women's experience of the masculine. I believe Linda Fierz-David is correct in her understanding that the women who were initiated in this chamber were given the opportunity to approach what, in myth, Ariadne achieved, i.e., rebirth and redemption and in Jungian terms, *wholeness*. She finds parallels between the drama depicted and the feminine journey of spiritual wholeness, what Jungian psychology would term today feminine *Individuation*.

The timeliness of the rediscovery of this chamber is indeed fortunate, as it brings coherence to the experience of contemporary women who undergo eruptions of the instinctual life in the psyche's effort to repel the patriarchal over-enculturation, which would diminish a woman's soul. The frescoes give meaning and suggest a way through, so that a woman may not lose hope when she undergoes the darkness of depression and the loss of connection with the various roles available to women in society.

The frescoes depict what occurs when old psychic structures give way (the women clothed) and buried instincts erupt (the mythological scenes and of terror and flagellation). There, one walks the razor's edge between madness and enlightenment, spiritual emergency or spiritual emergence. The symbolism of wine—its capacity to bring community and conviviality and to loosen consciousness, even leading toward the experience of the enspiritedness of Divinity, along with the real threat of inciting animalistic and mad behavior—all point to the possibilities offered by walking this razor's edge.

The frescoes depict the process and the possibility of successfully emerging from the trial of loss of ego identity to a greater sense of self. When we walk the course of the woman or women experiencing the Villa of Mysteries Initiation, we are privy to the experience of utter self-abnegation, loss (what Ariadne experienced as intense abandonment and rejection), the soul stripped bare of any defense and identity protection, symbolized by the clothes of one's culture as well as the loss of shoes—that which protect the feet and separate one from the natural state. The process depicted on the walls of the Initiation Chamber are intensely evocative of the suffering and pain in life that break open the known self (the ego, or "personality") in order to reveal the deeper, truer *Self*.

The women of 2000 years ago lived in a threshold moment, as we do today. A culture of rationality and materialism was taking hold and the perception of more fluid states of consciousness was dwindling. In the twenty-first century, we are on the other side of that de-velopment. Throughout the 2000 years between the women of that time and now, rationality and materialism have grown and matured to culminating development as well as the potential of their enrichment to psyche. We find ourselves, once again, at the bridge between two worlds, but standing now at the other side. The need is, once again, the same. While the psychic need then was to find a bridge between the natural and the civilized worlds, the psychic need of today is to find relationship between our individualized, civilized selves and the natural world, between rational and irrational states of consciousness, between masculine and feminine modes of perception, between our sense of *Self* as unique and valuable and our unity with the cosmos. What was a high priority then reemerges on the opposite side of the bridge spanning 2000 years.

Meanwhile, patriarchy has managed to obviate the psycho-spiritual path of women. There are no mysteries, at least none officially recognized, for women to find meaning in the passage of time experienced in their bodies and in psyche. There are no menstrual rites preparing young women for maturity, no marriage and childbirth passage rites, and certainly no sacred ceremonies honoring women entering elderhood. The rites in the Villa of Mysteries seem to have met the needs of mature women seeking meaning, after puberty, marriage, and childbirth.

In Greece, we have seen that Dionysian rites never failed to honor the mature woman. While it celebrated fecundity, certainly, the priestesses involved with the preparations for the sacred marriage rite in Athens were the *Gerarai*, the geriatric, older women, mature women. While lightning strikes the younger women in the call of sex, it strikes again as she makes the passage into the wisdom years. Lightning was ever associated with Dionysos, and the older woman literally experiences the lightning in the hot flashes, which we have been taught to interpret as a plague, just as young women were taught to call their monthly flow "the curse."

The Sacred Drama of Initiation as depicted in the Villa

So what is it that occurs in the tableau? What is the process depicted, the passage prescribed by Orphic/Dionysian wisdom?

The Vestibule

Just before entering the chamber, in the small vestibule (technically, what was called the *fauces*), there is a small temple-like structure in the corner. Small bones were discovered inside indicating a preliminary sacrifice. The essential meaning would be that prior to entrance into the mysteries, one would make an offering to the sacred. One would release something of value to one's ego in an act of reverence.

The Chamber

The First Scene—The Recitation

Entering the room, the nearest scene to the left, closest to the door and clearly the first in the series, depicts a woman in full Roman matronly dress, veiled, and apparently attentive to a young boy who is looking at a scroll and presumably reading aloud. Another woman, seated and holding another scroll, likewise, looks towards the boy, while yet another, walking away from the reader, turns slightly backwards, apparently also listening as she leaves the scene with a tray of cakes in her left hand and a sprig of greenery in her right.

> Everywhere in the world, a *teaching* belonged to initiation, which consisted of the ritual telling of sacred myths. The Greek word *mythologein* means just such a telling, through which the myth as word (Logos) can become alive in the heart of the listener. In this respect, the myth is the *theoria*, that is, the perception which brings about inner knowledge and forms the hypothesis of religious practice. The *theoria* of the Orphic cult was the myth of the horrible death of Zagreus (Dionysos) and of his rebirth, and it is obviously this myth which the boy in our scene has to read.[189]

---

[189] L. Fierz-David, *Dreaming in Red*, p. 42.

So, it is apparent that the feminine figures are attentive to the recitation of the *theoria* involved with what will occur. The naked boy child only wears *cothurni* (high laced boots associated in ancient Greece with Dionysos). The boots indicate the presence of Dionysos in the child.

There is considerable conjecture about the identities of the women, i.e., which are priestesses, who is the candidate for initiation, who is the High Priestess? To me, it appears that the first woman is the candidate, as well as the woman who moves into the second scene with the tray and greenery sprig. The various levels of dress and undress are particularly notable in the figures. Of all the figures in the room, the first is the most covered and clothed with the dress of her time and culture. As the initiation progresses (except for the woman who makes the preparation at the table in scene 2, and the woman who kneels before the *liknon* basket in scene 8, and the very final panel of scene 10), the women are quite simply dressed in tunics and a long piece of material that serves as a drape and in one scene, a cape. The costume of culture drops away to reveal simplicity and naturalness.

The woman moving forward, yet turning back slightly to listen while carrying the cakes, almost appears to be pregnant. Leopold Feiler, a doctor, noticed this as well, but on closer inspection he concluded that she is quite slim beneath the draping, the folds simply giving the appearance of pregnancy.[190] The artist may have been suggesting a pregnancy, not with a human child, but a soul preparing to give birth to a new self. The theme of mystery religions worldwide is death and rebirth on a spiritual level. The Egyptian mysteries, the Eleusinian mysteries, and the Dionysian mysteries all worked with this intention. Today's Rosicrucian and Masonic mysteries reiterate the same theme.

What do we learn from the action so far? That in order to move forward, one must approach with reverence, as symbolized by the

---

[190] L. Fierz-David, *Dreaming in Red*, p.43.

preliminary offerings; deeply listen for the Divine as depicted by the attentive listening to the *theoria*; and be willing to become a vessel for the Divine, symbolized by pregnancy.

The woman carries a tray of cakes. Cakes are made from flour, which of course derives from wheat, everywhere a symbol of the gifts of Mater, the Mother, Earth.[191] The cakes may be seen to represent our material body. This idea remains in the Catholic Mass, in which "the Host" made of wheat, represents the body of the Savior. The woman's head is crowned with ivy, signifying her dedication to Dionysos. Both her feet are shod in sandals.

She also carries a twig of greenery, which is thought to be a small branch of laurel.[192] Laurel is symbolic of achievement, courage, immortality, incorruptible love, purity, and victory after significant trials.[193] She carries the sprig in her right hand, the active and usually dominant hand. She carries the tray of sacrificial cakes on her left. Perhaps the gesture signifies a willing sacrifice, along with the active intention to successfully traverse the trial of the path of initiation in purity and love. Laurel was sacred to the god Apollo, Dionysos' counterpart. Perhaps this, in some way, is an honoring of the rational, solar side of consciousness even as she prepares to enter the depths of what has been unconscious. This interpretation, of course, was not so clear in that time and place, but ensuring that the complement (and opposite) of the god featured for devotion was also given tribute, would make sense both psychologically and ritually.

The Second Scene—Preparations

Where is she going? She moves towards a setting in which preparations are being made. Three ladies—priestesses—and one

---

[191] J.C. Cooper, *An Illustrated Encyclopaedia of Traditional Symbols*, p.43.

[192] Cooper, *An Illustrated Encyclopaedia of Traditional Symbols*, p. 43.

[193] G. Jobes, *Dictionary of Mythology, Folklore and Symbols, Part 2*, p. 976.

perhaps now representing the candidate, attend a central veiled and seated figure who lifts a purple drape with her left hand while looking to her right and holding the sprig beneath a stream of water being poured out by a woman with a scroll held in place by a belt at her waist. The scroll might be the *theoria,* or it might be a script for the ritual. The central woman's acts indicate ceremonial gestures that follow the offering. She is most likely the High Priestess. Because we see her from the back, what she is doing is mostly hidden from the viewer, surely intentionally. She appears to be veiling the object in the *liknon* basket we will encounter again in the seventh scene. The pouring out of water to her right is likely the offering of libation, which was a common gesture honoring the unseen powers. Purification might also be implied.

The Third Scene—Nature's Tranquility

What follows is an entire change in mood and locus. Now we find ourselves no longer in the human sphere, but in the realm of forest spirits. The central figure is Silenus, the traditional companion and tutor of Dionysos. Silenus was considered a very wise and profound spirit.[194] His name is the conjunction of two Greek words, *seilo* meaning "to and fro," and *lenos,* "wine trough." Thus, he was associated with the wine press, and specifically the actions needed to create the inspirited liquid. This might be an apt metaphor for the psychic process our postulant will undergo. In Plato's *Symposium,* the prominent Athenian general and statesman, Alcibiades, who studied with and greatly revered Socrates, compared his teacher with Silenus. As Linda Fierz-David notes, the features of Silenus in our chamber look a great deal like Socrates. Thus, a deep wisdom will propel the next phase of the

---

[194] Larousse, *World Mythology,* p. 139.

candidate's journey. And it is this deep wisdom that will challenge and test her.

Silenus is an *animus* figure of wisdom, a guide and mentor, who begins the real induction into the realm of spirit, as symbolized by the playing of the lyre. This instrument is specifically associated with Orpheus (Orphism is the source of this Dionysian rite). The music of Orpheus was said to have been so sweet that it tamed wild beasts and moved even in*anima*te objects. In playing the lyre, Silenus acts as a representative for Orpheus. And his soft, feminine corpulence indicates a connection with the Earth Mother as well as a certain androgyny, echoing the androgynous characteristics of Dionysos and supporting the theme of Integration in our understanding of both Dionysos and Ariadne in their sacred marriage. Linda Fierz-David notes,

> ...Silenus is perhaps to be compared with those medicine men of primitive tribes who wore women's clothing and pretended to be women just at the time when their function was a spiritual, guiding, teaching one.[195]

Alongside Silenus, perched on rocky terrain, sit a panisk and a faun. They appear docile and sweet. One plays pipes, associated with the great god Pan, indicative of a call for his presence. The panisk who appears to be male nurses a kid, a young goat (an animal, as we have explored, strongly associated with Dionysos). The mood is the placid and most lovely side of nature.

The Fourth & Fifth Scene—Terror

The candidate surely was inducted into that gentle mood when all at once the tranquility is violently disrupted. We know this by the return of a woman in the tableau, turning away vehemently from what

---

[195] L. Fierz-David, *Dreaming in Red,* p. 60

is coming, with a warding-off gesture and expression of focused concern. Her violet drape billows out with her momentum like a sail, indicating the speed of her retreat. What has frightened her so? The wall ends and is met now by the furthest wall in the room, what would be considered the *Holy of Holies,* the *Sanctum Sanctorum,* of the chamber. At the end, closest to the terrified woman, we find Silenus again (in the Fifth Scene) in the company of two male youths with goat's ears. Silenus looks towards the woman with a stern expression and holds a jug, presumed to be filled with wine, into which one of the youths intently gazes, while the other holds a grotesque mask parodying the features of Silenus overhead. It would seem that that mask is reflected in the wine. Is it this mask that terrifies the woman? I spent five days with these images, and it was only on the last day that the intent of the mask became suddenly apparent. The mask is the face of madness. Behind it threatens a frightening emptiness, an abyss. The spirit of Dionysos, present in the wine, threatens insanity. The Arcadian scene, which lulled the woman into self-forgetfulness, and a loosening of consciousness, now presents its shadow. If she is successful in her initiation pilgrimage, she will achieve transcendence. If not, she could fall into psychosis. The Dionysian way is not a path for the weak or squeamish.

The Sixth Scene—The Divine Couple

At the very center of this far wall are the central figures of Dionysos and Ariadne. It has been argued that the female figure might be Semele, his mother; however, the presence of a wedding ring on her hand draped gently over his shoulder seems definitive proof that this is his bride, not his mother. Unfortunately, her upper body is missing because of damage to the wall. But her strength is evident from her stable seated posture. Her love radiates from that gentle hand around her lover's neck. Dionysos, in a state of complete repose, leans against her. His legs fall open at an angle, which indicate complete trust and utter relaxation. One foot is bare and the other shod. He looks up adoringly at her. Their figures are uninvolved with the action that surrounds them and loom larger than the others, indicating that though they are the *raison d'être* of the entire proceedings, they rest beyond them. At the center of the wall representing the deepest mystery, the spiritual goal, the *coniunctio,* the *sacred marriage.*

As noted earlier, it is of supreme significance that Ariadne does not lean upon him, the god, but the other way around. He becomes part of her, not she of him. This indicates that he is the spiritual creative spark that she incorporates into her own soul, becoming in that process a whole, empowered, inspired, and deeply feminine woman. Her creative process is inseminated by the divine masculine, promising a fertile creativity to her soul. She does not own him, but he leans into her being. Like the "Woman Clothed with the Sun" of the Biblical Book of Revelation, Ariadne is metaphorically clothed with him, her source of light, and experiences radiance. She becomes Aridella, "the bright and shining," "all clear" one. In the image, her one foot is bare and the other sandaled, as are his. This divine couple transcends all boundaries. They walk between worlds and, as a result of her reverence for them, so ultimately, will the Initiate. In the process of her initiation, she must descend to transcend, and integrate.

This is the goal of our candidate for initiation. She must release her ties to society and return to a natural innocence and purity, dissolving all sense of personal identity and the accoutrements of *persona.* And she must face the terrors which dissolution of ego presents. She must make herself vulnerable not only to the beautiful and gentle, but also to the terror of the unknown, and to the possible demons that lurk in the depths of psyche, if she is to come into real contact with the numinous powers of Nature and the Divine. She must risk all, by her willingness to undergo complete naked vulnerability, as her model and queen Ariadne did, if she hopes to achieve her holy union.

The Seventh Scene—The Cista Mystica

At this point in the progression of scenes, one can safely assume the woman in this scene is the candidate undergoing initiation. Linda Fierz-David received the strong impression that the terrified woman depicted in the fourth scene was in the act of stepping out of the tableau. She imagined her descending to the crypt below the Villa where utter darkness at first prevails.[196] Only after many steps, taken gingerly as one steps forward in that underground passage, does a small shaft of light appear. I have been down there and experienced it. It is so dark in the middle of the day that absolutely nothing is visible for a surprisingly long time. She imagined that the woman descended there on her mission to retrieve the *liknon*, a boat-like basket used commonly for threshing and also carrying newborn infants in ancient Greece, but used in a sacred manner to carry the holy emblem of the god (the phallos) in his festivals. It is certainly possible that the woman, during her initiation, would be required to descend and experience total darkness.

That darkness would represent the total annihilation of rational mind and utter surrender to death—at least of the ego and everything this woman had considered herself to be, and to have achieved up to this point in her life. The *Thyades* of ancient Greece annually undertook a similar perilous journey in the dead of winter to retrieve the newborn god from the sacred cave. The foot of the fleeing woman is, indeed, stepping forward and slightly out of the panel. The mood is one of terror, making a descent into darkness that much more plausible, at least symbolically. She reappears at last in the seventh scene. She is now in the *Holy of Holies*, on the central panel, adjacent to the right of the larger-than-life portraits of Dionysos and Ariadne.

She is now barefoot, wears a saffron headband, and her hair is tied up. On her knees, with a large stick (partially damaged in the

---

[196] L. Fierz-David, *Dreaming in Red,* p. 77.

fresco) across her shoulder, which I interpret to be a *thyrsus* (Linda Fierz-David believes it to be an extinguished torch), she kneels before a boat-shaped basket, unanimously believed by scholars to be a Dionysian *liknon*. Something quite large stands within this basket, covered by a purple drape. Based on the evidence of the Dionysian celebrations in ancient Greece discussed earlier, this would be the hidden *phallos* of the god. It is unclear exactly what she is doing with the drape, but Linda Fierz-David is convinced, and probably rightly, that she is about to uncover the prize retrieved from the depths.

Her cap particularly interests me, as no detail in such scenes is ever random. I found only one reference, which mentions "the mystic headband" of initiates in the Greek mysteries.[197] It would seem she is wearing that special accoutrement and now carries the special staff of a dedicated follower of the god. She has accomplished retrieval of the *cista mystica* (mystic container). Behind her stand two other women, one of whom carries a tray with what appears to be pine needles lying in a bundle. The pine, as we have seen in the analysis of the pinecone that sits atop the *thyrsus*, is sacred to Dionysos. It is evergreen even in the coldest winter frost. It represents ongoing life despite serious threat of death posed in the dark of winter. The later Christian incarnation of this same theme is the Christmas tree decorated with lights in December. As we have seen, Dionysos is *Zoë*, the force of life itself, life that resurrects and is never fully conquered by death. The priestess' tray with the pine needle branches is positioned above the head of the lady who is on her knees, fully focused on the basket and its content. Life and light has triumphed over darkness.

When all seems to have concluded with successful result, however, all hell breaks loose, literally! From the darkest depths of the unconscious and superconscious rises the lightning flash of Dionysos, in the form of the dark-winged angel. She stands erect in high

---

[197] M. B. Cosmopoulos, *Greek Mysteries: The Archaeology of Ancient Greek Secret Cults*, p. 125.

Dionysian cothurni boots, a sure sign of the presence of Dionysos, and is about to flick a large whip onto the bare back of the woman in the following panel. While her body is mostly at the edge of the seventh scene, her gaze and the intent of her action is towards the following panel on the adjacent wall. What has the woman done to deserve this response from the transcendent heights represented by the wings, and the unconscious depths represented by their darkness?

Renowned Italian archaeologist and foremost authority on the frescoes, Amedeo Maiuri, believed the angel to be Aidos, the Greek goddess of shame, modesty, humility, and reverence. She assists humanity to do right and to avoid transgressions. If this is so, the woman was probably about to commit a sacrilege by lifting the veil. Though she may retrieve it in her own nature and may recover it from the dark depths, she can never *possess* the divine creative spark represented by the *phallos*. She cannot ever fully know or own the masculine, just as a man can never fully fathom the feminine. But she can orient herself in proper relationship to it. She can prepare the holy ground of her soul for him, but she must never inflate psychically to hubris, which in all cases leads to disaster. The angel, in fact, rescues our heroine from that fatal mistake. The temptation to inflation, which would have spelled utter defeat, just as it did in the case of Icarus and his wings as he flew towards the Sun, is prevented at the last moment by the angel of reverence and modesty on behalf of the god.

The crack of this whip would strike like Dionysian lightning, shattering the ego's pretensions. Pride is always the last and most dangerous test on the path of initiation. This is literally so. Many spiritual exemplars have tumbled as a result of hubris. Ego prevents the passage into true evolutionary achievement. The ego believes it has accomplished the great deed, when in truth divine visitation and advancement is always a grace bestowed, and never on demand. The best we humans can do is simply prepare, "set the table" so to speak, cleansing and readying the psyche, while cultivating virtue.

The Eighth Scene—The Flagellation

Here we find our candidate fully subjugating herself to the will of heaven, seen here as the whip of the dark-winged Dionysian Angel. She lays her head, eyes cast downward, hair dishevelled, in the lap of a priestess, who with one hand holds her head and with the other bares the back of our still barefoot postulant. The attending priestess looks towards the angel, clearly in solemn service. Ego has deflated. The postulant, in her utter surrender, is victorious.

> At the point of vulnerability is where the surrender takes place—that is where the god enters.[198]

We know this has occurred because immediately following we see her dancing fully nude. Her lovely figure is viewed from the rear, as if to say: this is not a mystery to be profaned by gawking. And one might notice that her back bears no wounds. She is entirely healed. She is the quintessence of feminine grace and joy. She holds the cymbals, sacred to Cybele, the divine feminine, above her head.[199] The movement of her scarf, which is her only clothing, billows out in such a way that it suggests she is dancing in a circular motion. The circle we have seen represents wholeness and is a symbol for the *Self.* A fully clothed priestess, holding a *thyrsus,* stands behind her in attendance. The scene is perhaps the most lovely of the entire sequence. And it is particularly powerful in contrast to the utter devastation of the previous panel. It is as if she has lost it all, but then comes the miraculous epiphany, just as Ariadne experienced on Naxos. She experienced psychic death. but in the dying she was reborn in the arms of the god.

There is a large window in the wall that follows this scene. Perhaps the sound effects that accompanied the ritual were produced outside this window? Was it draped for the ceremony and then opened

---

[198] M. Woodman, *Conscious Femininity*, p. 32.

[199] G. Jobes, *Dictionary of Mythology, Folklore and Symbols, Part 1*, p, 402.

to reveal the natural light at a certain moment? We have no answers, but having experienced a well-orchestrated initiation ceremony myself, music and sound effects were a valuable and powerful induction to the senses. Sound was very much a part of the Dionysian experience and specifically choreographed in Euripides' *Bacchae* to indicate the approach and presence of the god. This opening in the wall would have allowed for that sort of orchestration while not filling up the space needed for the ritual in the room. This, of course, is simply my conjecture. I overheard a guide argue that no initiation ceremony occurred in this room, as evinced by the large window. I cannot agree. These intricate purposeful panels could not be purely decorative. The presence of the large window doesn't discount the possibility of religious ritual and rites being practiced there.

The Ninth Scene—The Return

The ceremony is complete. Our Initiate prepares to return to the world. She is assisted in arranging her long tresses by another woman. She gazes towards the viewer with gentle seriousness, as if to say, "*I know.*" She has experienced "gnosis," the knowing that permeates the cells on a molecular level and brooks no doubt, a knowing that far surpasses idea and belief, as well as simply reason. Her knowing includes the supra-rational, a deeply felt sense of truth, because she has experienced it.

A young *erote* holds up a mirror. The assistant priestess gazes towards the mirror, but our Initiate seems unaware or at least, uninterested. It is difficult to tell whose reflection is seen in the small rectangular space. This small detail led me to wonder if indeed the two women are sides of one woman—she who minds the details of life and does well to self-reflect from time to time and she who belongs to the god, the mystic. With that perspective, I looked back at the series of double figures of women on this side of the room. An argument could be made that each pair reflects two aspects of the woman; one, the receptive mystic initiate, and the other, an officiant who actively serves the process. The difference in dress is especially noticeable between the dancing maiden and her attendant, who seems to be dressed in formal clothing, which might be properly worn at a social function within Pompeii society. And yet she carries the *thyrsus* as the maiden dances with the cymbals. While the Initiate fully expresses her liberated femininity, the clothed attendant looks towards the preceding scene, holding the emblem of Dionysian allegiance, and as we have discovered, the *thyrsus* wand, signifying enlightenment.

Before we leave the ninth scene, it feels valuable to point out the mirroring theme that has repeated in the sequence. The first mirror was in the third scene, represented by the jug of wine held up by Silenus to reflect the more dreadful face of all things Dionysian. Mythically, the mirror, it will be remembered, is deeply meaningful as the toy the young Dionysos became fascinated by — and thus distracted — so that he is was easily surrounded and torn to pieces by the Titans. Self-reflection is dangerous, but it is essential in the Dionysian path of ego death and spiritual rebirth. The mirror returns in the tableau, held up by an *erote* in this ninth scene as if to say, *love has made possible the new wholeness and beauty you have achieved within.*

Just to the side, on the short wall facing the seated woman with her attendant in the ninth scene, is another *erote* who stands, gazing up at the seated woman, bow in hand, no arrow visible. Has his arrow met its mark? The arrow of divine love has completed its task of wedding the Initiate to the god, of establishing the wholeness only love can accomplish. His weight rests on his left leg over which his right gently rests. The left side of the body is traditionally associated with the feminine and the feminine qualities of receptivity and relatedness upon which this whole process revolves. Both *erotes,* in fact, carry the weight on their left leg. His right arm is propped on a ledge and his chin rests on that fist. His left hand holds the bow.

The Tenth Scene—The Domina

We come now to the tenth and final scene on the other side of the wide entrance. It is easy to miss, just as the final *erote* is, flanking the large entrance on two short walls that face inwards towards the room. Here sits what Maiuri and other writers call the *Domina*. The *Domina* would be the mistress of the Villa, and in terms of the mysteries, its supreme High Priestess.

Another interpretation is offered by Linda Fierz-David. She imagines the *Domina* as the embodiment of *Mnemosyne,* memory.[200] *Mnemosyne* was the mother of the muses and the grandmother of Orpheus. She was also the patroness of poets and of the masters of the oral traditions. Fierz-David points out that this is the only figure who looks towards Dionysos and Ariadne, and seems to survey the whole process from her comfortable armchair. This is a plausible interpretation, as Orphism highly venerated the faculty of memory. It was believed that if a person could remember their lives and the instructions given to them to prepare for the afterlife, they could go on to the Elysian Fields and not be required to return to a new incarnation. Specifically, it was considered valuable to remember the details of initiation. An Orphic invocation to Mnemosyne reads,

> "Excite the initiates with the memory of the pious ritual
> and send oblivion away from them."[201]

Mnemosyne, ensuring the Initiate will remember the instructions given in the ritual, acts as their protector and soul guide. It was said that if people sat upon the throne of *Mnemosyne,* they could remember all that they had learned in life. The armchair in the panel might be *Mnemosyne's* throne.

---

[200] L. Fierz-David, *Dreaming in Red,* p. 146.

[201] R. G. Edmond, (Ed.), *The 'Orphic' Gold Tablets and the Greek Religion: Further Along the Path,* p. 75.

A simpler explanation might be that the seated lady is the Initiate herself. Having integrated the ritual, and having achieved the inner marriage, she quietly surveys the chamber and gazes knowingly towards the goal of the *coniunctio* with quiet dignity and authority. In contrast to the fully covered woman appearing in the first panel dressed in full Roman matronly apparel, the final panel presents a similarly veiled woman, but in a far more relaxed and open manner. The *Domina's* presence silently speaks balance, strength, clarity, and soul maturity. These virtues would be the fruit of the trials and ecstasy of the initiation process and a deepened understanding of life and death.

Conclusion

The journey depicted in the Villa of Mysteries illustrates, in Dionysian metaphor, the psychological process of any woman who ventures on a depth process of *self*-knowledge, *Integration* and *Individuation*. The priestesses who assist the postulant in the present day might take the form of a wise analyst or psychotherapist who "has been there" and is able to hold steady for the client. Being witnessed and having the containment of the therapeutic or analytic hour serves as a sort of initiatory chamber, in which the woman is assisted by a person who can walk the path with her because she or he knows and trusts the journey and the goal.

Sometimes a woman has to go the way alone. This is when journaling is an especially useful tool as a mirror of self-reflection. Creative self-expression and reading literature also help point the way, bolstering faith in the journey. Art, especially, can transform a psychological situation. Profoundly wise Jungian analyst Marion Woodman explains to one of her interviewers, Rachel V.:

> Unless an incident is made conscious, it does not happen to the soul. It has to be thought about, written about, painted, danced, made into music. In other

words, it must move from literal to metaphoric if it is to assimilate into the soul's flowering.[202]

Ritual does this, and art does this. She further explains that the root meaning for metaphor is "to transform." The metaphor acts as a transformer of the raw energy patterns into forms, which can be assimilated by consciousness.[203] The Pompeii ritual was rich in transformative metaphor, and thus had a real potential to assist the woman to reach her goal safely.

As we peer across the bridge spanning two thousand years, we realize that there was wisdom in the ways of that earlier epoch. Therapy has gradually been moving from a focus on healing neuroses– basically, the issues emerging from the deficits of childhood– to the concerns of *Individuation* and soul growth. In addition, we would do well to rediscover the real benefits of ritual, which has mostly been thrown out as a reaction to mistrust of religious authority, as well as a focus on reason. However, the psychological and spiritual benefits are rich. Perhaps it is time for women and men to rediscover healing and transformative ritual, both experienced on their own and in the fellowship of trusted others. Carefully and intuitively constructed, ritual heals and elevates.

[202] M. Woodman, *Conscious Femininity*, p. 52.

[203] Woodman, *Conscious Femininity*, p. 54.

PART THREE

DIONYSOS AND ARIADNE IN TODAY'S WORLD

THE WORLD

11

DIONYSOS AND THE FEMININE IN THE CONTEMPORARY WORLD

As we have discovered, Dionysos and the feminine are intrinsically related. This relationship begins with the myth wherein Dionysos is liberated from madness inflicted by Hera, wife of Zeus, the supreme god on Mount Olympus. Hera is the quintessential archetype of "Wife." She finds fulfillment in that classic role. In reaction to the humiliation of her husband's affair with Dionysos' mother, Semele, Hera succeeds at last in discovering Dionysos' whereabouts and curses him with madness.

Hera might be seen to represent the effect of patriarchy on the feminine. A daughter of patriarchy, she finds the center of her existence and her life's meaning in her husband, who tragically does not show her the same respect. But here is the twist to the story: Rhea, the mother of Hera, removes Hera's curse and initiates Dionysos into her mysteries. Rhea, as the Titaness mother goddess, predates the Olympians and is far older than patriarchy. While Hera rules Mt. Olympus — and the other mother goddess, Demeter, rules the abundance of the cultivated earth — Rhea is associated with rocky, wild untamed terrain. Rhea is the Earth Mother *before* the civilizing effect of agriculture. Dionysos is persecuted by a Patriarchal (solar phallic) version of the feminine and rescued by an untamed, eternal feminine essence, which endures in spite of the civilizing forces that overtook her reign.

Before encountering Rhea, while still a child, he is disguised as a girl to avoid detection by Hera. He learns the ways of girls in order to survive. And he longs to know his true mother, Semele, who died before his birth. After his cure from insanity, he ultimately braves the Underworld to find and retrieve her. He then discovers his soulmate in Ariadne, a mortal who has also known loneliness and betrayal and whose soul, likewise, refuses domestication. Dionysos is always and everywhere identified with freedom. One of his familiar epithets in Roman times was *Liber*, the god of freedom.[204]

The important corollary between Dionysos and the feminine, as well as the value of *liberty*, reveals itself in the progression of modern culture. In reviewing the history of the rights of women in the 18th-21st centuries, a very interesting pattern emerges. Feminism, a term coined in the late 1800s in France (*féminisme*), has been identified by Feminists and Women's Studies scholars as having *Three Waves*.

The Three Waves of Feminism

The *First Wave* was focused on gaining full rights for women, and came on the heels of the *Abolitionist Movement* that had been spearheaded by *women* to abolish slavery. Finding resistance to their voices on account of being women, the issue of women's rights then came to the forefront. Before the *First Wave,* no woman could own property, execute wills or sign legal documents, serve on juries—even on trials of women-- vote in elections, refuse sex to her husband, go to college, have legal custody of her children, or divorce her husband. Alice Paul, Elizabeth Cady Stanton, Susan B. Anthony, Ida B. Wells, Lucretia Mott, and others in the nineteenth and early twentieth century spoke out with great courage to gain freedom and to establish women's rights. Christian teachings were scrutinized regarding the oppression and inequality of women. *The Woman's Bible* (1895) written by Elizabeth Cady Stanton and a committee of 26 women, challenged the

---

[204] C. Kerényi, *Dionysos*, p. 375.

traditional position of religious orthodoxy that women should be subservient to men. Stanton wanted to break free of doctrinal shackles and promote a liberating theology that stressed self-development. Florence Nightingale established female nurses as adjuncts to the military. The first birth control clinic was opened in 1916 by Margaret Sanger, a radical act even now, giving women authority to make choices regarding their own bodies and their future. Meanwhile, World War I (1914-1918) brought many women into the work force for the first time.

When considering what else was occurring in the culture during the *First Wave*, with an eye to the Dionysian lens, I was amazed to realize that *prohibition* was likewise an issue of the day. Alcohol, in all cases, even in its rejection, calls forth a Dionysian focus. Thus, we see that *freedom, women's issues, and alcohol* (emblematic of substances that affect consciousness) were all concerns at that historical juncture.

The *Second Wave* rolled in as the *Women's Liberation* movement in the 1960s, accompanying the *Civil Rights Movement* and the struggle to end the war in Vietnam. The pendulum that had swung to complete abstinence from alcohol from 1920-1933 (the law anyway), now swung to its opposite pole with near veneration for "sex, drugs, and rock n' roll," facilitated by the invention of the Pill and the emergence of "flower power." We find a plethora of Dionysians in the rock bands of the era, and many casualties of the "too muchness" of an unbridled era. But liberties too were won. The *Civil Rights Act* was passed in 1964, outlawing discrimination based on race, color, religion, sex, or national origin. Women's issues, for the first time, found legitimized academic standing in universities. Though still greatly underrepresented, women did at last enter politics and the workplace in managerial and administrative positions.

Now we find ourselves in what Rebecca Walker called the *Third Wave*.[205] Rebecca, the daughter of Alice Walker, author of *The Color*

---

[205] R. Walker, *Ms. Magazine*, 1992.

Purple, and a White, Jewish-American father, Mel Leventhal, identifies herself as "Black, White, and Jewish." Her mother, Alice, had already written regarding the inequity between White women who naturally enjoy cultural privilege in a White society and Women of Color in the feminist movement. Alice Walker coined the term *Womanist*, which is specifically concerned with the perspectives and voices of Women of Color.[206] *Womanism* intentionally includes the word "man," recognizing that Black men are a part of Black women's lives as family, including children, lovers, and friends.

There is a balance here that was lacking in the earlier feminist agendas, which mostly held an ambivalent if not antagonistic view of men. In this way, *Womanism* is more in line with the pattern we have been exploring of women and Dionysos. *Womanism* distinguishes between Black women's and White women's experience of men. In addition, it intentionally honors the sexual power of Black women without ignoring a history of sexual violence. What is unique about *Womanism* is that it is not concerned with politics and a value system, but is focused specifically on honoring the strength and experience of Black women. The internet discussion on *Womanism* tends to include all Women of Color, not only Black women, as all WOCs have experienced marginalization in the culture. It does purposefully exclude White women, in order to specifically honor the voice of women who ordinarily would be shouted over by White women's views and concerns.

Rebecca Walker's work includes the *Womanist* values her mother highlighted, while extending those concerns to women in general and incorporating political concerns. In 1992, at age 22, she wrote an article in response to the result of the hearings over the issue of sexual harassment by Clarence Thomas. His appointment to the Supreme Court was confirmed. Rebecca Walker, in protest, wrote a

---

[206] A. Walker, *In Search of Our Mothers' Gardens:* Prose.

powerful article which declared at the close, "I am not a post-feminist. I am the *Third Wave.*"

The *Second Wave* brought significant strides in terms of women's rights in academia and in the workplace. However, as we have seen, a growing awareness of the inequities between White women and Women of Color ensued and that has expanded into an ever-broadening field of concern that spans gender, class, color, and extends into the arts, culture, as well as power and politics. *Third Wave* concerns outpace the concerns of the *Second Wave*, in its inclusiveness. Whereas the *First* and *Second Waves* were mostly focused on redefining the *roles* of women, the *Third Wave* has been concerned with understanding and expanding notions of *gender*. These developments fall into line with the fluidity of the archetype of Dionysian gender identity.

With this *Third Wave*, the LGBTQ movement has arisen. Same-sex marriage and transgender rights make the headlines. In Dionysian fashion, *androgyny* makes its appearance even in unisex names now quite commonly given to our babies. Marijuana is becoming legalized, and though still illegal, psychoactive substances are easily available for shamanic psycho-spiritual journeys. On the religious front, we have never had such free access to the esoteric and mystical teachings of East and West. And last, but by no means least, there is universal concern about caring for the earth and addressing the concerns of global warming, the systemic functioning of the environment, as well as methods of agribusiness.

As we can see, concerns with women's rights and the Dionysian current, which strongly advocates *freedom* (whether it be political, religious or mystical) are inseparable threads. In addition, there is a growing awareness of everyone's natural mother, the Earth. While the *First* and *Second Wave* were polarized in their Dionysian expression—as evinced by prohibition in the *First Wave,* and the license of the 1960s in the *Second Wave* — we have a profound opportunity with this ongoing *Third Wave.*

This new opportunity is to find a growing *Integration* and inclusiveness that honors women and men of all colors and persuasions, recognizes diversity, and yet holds as central our essential unity as the family of humanity and our relationship and responsibility to the mother of life, the Earth, as well as to our own physical bodies.

12

A Contemporary View
Dionysos and Ariadne in the 21ˢᵀ Century

How do the living currents of Dionysos and Ariadne express themselves personally and in our relationships? In this chapter we will consider how Dionysos finds expression in masculine psychology, and how to identify the presence of Ariadne in the feminine soul. In conclusion, we will look at the remarkable Dionysian currents in contemporary culture and how they emerge always in tandem with the concerns of women and the values of freedom and equality.

Dionysian Signs and Symptoms

- *Freedom,* an essential requirement. (*"Liber"* was Dionysos' epithet in Rome). A strong will and refusal to be confined or categorically defined.
- *Egalitarian* (non elitist)
- *Individuality* as a predominant value, rather than conformity
- Respect and admiration for *the feminine*: love of wife, mother, and the earth
- Ease with gender fluidity: *bisexuality and trans-sexuality, non binary identity*
- Luxuriating in the *Senses*
- Love of *Nature;* appreciation of the *wild and untamed.*
- Love of *Beauty,* aesthetics—both found in Nature and that which is fashioned through art

- Appreciation of music, drums and rhythmic beat
- High value placed on *relating*
- *Feeling* situations, rather than analyzing
- *Mystical* temperament
- *Shamanic* gifts—comfortable in the in-between places (*liminality*)—and with the bloodiness of birth, of sex, death, and all transitions
- Ability to *let loose, let go*, surrender. Orgasmic.
- Drawn to *the depths of things, situations, people*
- *Oracular* interests, and sometimes gifts (can accurately perform divination)
- *Self-reflection* (as evinced by the mirror in his Orphic mysteries) even at the cost of psychological "*dismemberment*," in the service of transformation
- Understands the value of *sacrifice for renewal*
- High value placed on *Imagination*
- Ability to *disguise* one's presence, and if needed, to become *invisible* in a crowd
- Recognition that *personae are worn as needed*, but not one's essential identity. Able to *release personae easily*…(as evidenced by *masks*, in his worship and celebration)
- Often an *Oenophile*—wine lover
- Able to *hold opposites*. Complex. Never boring or one-dimensional.
- Possible attraction to, omens/dreams of one or more of the following: *Pines, Ivy, Vines, Forests, Honey, Wild Cats* (especially panthers, tigers), which exemplify grace and untamed power, Bulls, Goats, Serpents, the *jewel colors* (burgundy, amethyst, forest green, lapis); *labyrinths, storms, and lightning*
- Comfortable in and with the *Dark*

The Dionysian in Dreams

These themes and images are not consigned to the distant past, but are living currents, experienced by women and men living in contemporary culture. They can occur on either side of the mirror of waking and sleeping time. A dream that provides an example in light of what we have discovered in the Villa of Mysteries, was dreamt by a white female client who had recently left a troubled marriage to a domineering spouse:

The dreamer finds herself on a healing table being tended by an African woman in traditional dress. The material of the healer's dress and head wrapping are a deep carnelian red with gold flecks in the print. The healer is concluding the session and gives the dreamer a paper bag, which the dreamer knows contains a penis. In some way, this possession will benefit the dreamer, but she has the impression she should take it with her and not open the bag.

The scene shifts and the dreamer now find herself on a plateau overlooking the sea at either sunrise or sunset. The dreamer does not know which. The sun is rosy red on the horizon. The dreamer wakes.

The client subsequently experienced the end of a passionate love affair, which she described as a sort of death experience. In its wake, however, she made major life decisions in which she relocated from an urban to a rural environment, evocative of Dionysian values, and shifted her occupation. Like the Initiate in the Villa, the dreamer was given the *phallos*, the essential symbol of masculine power, which she instinctively knew she should revere as a gift, and not dishonor as a possession. These changes vastly improved her living situation and had a significantly impact upon her future.

The theme of the *phallos* in the *Liknon* basket, the subsequent symbolic flagellation experienced in her life by the devastating end to the love affair, and the rosy sunset/dawn over the ocean (waters of consciousness) might be interpreted as the death and rebirth this woman needed to experience to come into maturity and a greater wholeness.

The following dream was dreamt by another woman. Though both partners were still living in the same house, divorce was imminent and the couple no longer shared the same bed. The woman had described her situation as repressive, and her husband as emotionally volatile and verbally abusive.

The dreamer finds herself with a number of others in a large room, sitting on the floor, in a circle, around a very large citrine crystal. The client notices her legs are stretched out in front of her and that there are a pair of male legs alongside hers. She has been sitting with her back against this man, between his legs. What is particularly noticeable is that instead of feet, he has hooves. She turns her head to look at him and he is a young, dark-haired, attractive man. She thinks, 'Oh, it's Pan!'"

Though the Dreamer defines the figure as Pan behind her, he definitely resonates with Dionysos, having often been found in Dionysos' retinue. The dreamer did not know the meaning of the citrine crystal but researched and found a description that rang true for her. Citrines, she discovered, were said to repel all negative energy, to have the ability to lift the psyche out of a difficult situation, and never need "cleansing." As she was living in a house that felt quite toxic to her and with a man who outwardly appeared conservative yet displayed wildness only in destructive fashion, this dream implied the *positive* support of a masculine wildness in making this life transition.

Recognizing the Dionysian Boy, Adolescent, and Man in an Apollonic World

A boy who is naturally Dionysian by temperament has a hard go of it in a culture with fixed and narrow ideas of what it means to be a man. Dionysian boys feel deeply and are naturally sensitive. Our culture tends to question and even ridicule a Dionysian boy's natural inclinations, and he suffers terribly when shamed. Typically, he is drawn to beauty and to the arts and mystical experiences, whether they be through the senses, in nature, or in church. Unless another archetype has added influence, he has no particular interest in competitive sports. If he pursues athletics, it is for the joy of the body—exploring its potential. A more likely choice would be individual activities like martial arts, which has the added incentive of a spiritual substratum, or fencing, which has a romantic flare. The Dionysian boy is intrigued by fairytales, myths, and accounts of chivalry. There is poetry in his soul. Dionysos is after all, resonant to the poet, Orpheus.

> If a parent has stereotyped expectations of what a boy should be interested in—rough-housing, mechanical interests, and sports—then a Dionysus boy who follows his own interest will probably be told, in one way or another, that he's behaving "like a girl." Little Dionysus gravitates toward what the women are doing because he loves to use his five senses—he wants his world to be full of sensual experience. He likes the feel of silk and fur, is interested in colors, can be enraptured by music. The kitchen, with its smells and tastes, is much more interesting to him than the garage. The theater is infinitely more fascinating than the ball park, clothes are more captivating than computers. These natural interests usually invite others to call him a "sissy," for acting like a sister—a girl.[207]

Adolescence is an especially critical time for everyone, but especially for the Dionysian male. He may fall in love intensely, with girls, boys, or both. Drug experimentation and alcohol are all a razor's edge as he seeks transcendent experiences. The requirements of education and work usually suffer. If he is fortunate enough to have an

---

[207] J. Shinoda Bolen, *Gods in Everyman,* pp. 262, 263.

early foundation that supports him, i.e., parents who accept and honor his gifts and differences, and the container within which he finds himself (his environment) is flexible enough to allow him adequate freedom while providing enough safety, he will be able to navigate towards positive *Self*-discovery. Jungian analyst Jean Shinoda Bolen recognizes the liability involved in the here-and-now perspective of the Dionysian temperament:

> ...since Dionysus lives in the immediate present, he needs to be patiently taught to consider today what comes due tomorrow, as well as what and how to learn from past experience (lessons he otherwise often fails to apply.)[208]

It comes as no surprise that when grown, Dionysian men tend towards creative self-expression. Drama, art, music, feeling-based writing, whether poetry or prose, that moves the reader, winemaking and the culinary arts, even floral arranging, express Dionysos. Beauty is usually a high priority and the enjoyment of the senses. Our culture doesn't greatly reward these talents; but there are lucky Dionysians who do succeed quite well when their talents are nurtured and find an appreciative audience. Jean Shinoda Bolen's work in her two books, the *Gods in Everyman* and *Goddesses in Everywoman*, explains that typically we have more than one archetype at play in our nature. Balancing the Dionysian traits with just enough of Apollo, Hermes, Hephaestus, or Zeus, for example, can help a man to actualize more effectively professionally and personally. Another remedy can be the assistance of a wife or of other people who have those traits—a common remedy in the artist world, in which artists are notorious for their poor business and marketing skills.

---

[208] Shinoda Bolen, *Gods in Everyman*, p. 265.

Famous Dionysians in the music world include Jim Morrison, Mick Jagger, Keith Richards, George Harrison, Jimmy Page, The Grateful Dead, David Bowie, and Prince. Some examples in the literary world have been D. H. Lawrence, Henry Miller, the playwright and screenwriter Sam Shepard, and the poet Dylan Thomas. In the arts, Salvador Dali and many of the Surrealists and expressionists express him. Actor Russell Brand, a wild man with a taste for esoteric mysticism, qualifies.

Tragically, many Dionysians don't traverse midlife well, because they have failed to integrate qualities more natural to other archetypes, like planning ahead. They tend to hold on to youth when it becomes inappropriate, and sometimes don't make it past middle age owing to overindulgence in substances, which now show long-term effects on the body and mind. There are some who, learning the art of consciousness, navigate the passage gracefully, expressing the best of Dionysos and tempering the dangers.

What best determines the fate of the Dionysian male, and Ariadne, for that matter, is sufficient "ego strength" and an interest in achieving wisdom. By "ego strength" I mean, the ability to self-reflect. Self-reflection is the ability to witness what is occurring along with one's reaction to it internally, then pause, and moderate a response. In the Orphic mysteries, Dionysos' favorite toy was the mirror, even when it led to temporary psychic fragmentation. Self-reflection accompanies the Dionysian archetype as a very real gift.

In observing one's reactions to what one experiences, there is a necessary fragmentation. One becomes two—at least—in the noticing. The *self*-witness or observer often can detect multiple parts of the *self*-involved in any reaction if she or he takes the time. And it is this witness who decides and wills how to respond, not simply react. Without an internal witness, one is at the mercy of one's emotional and instinctual reactions.

We have seen the great power of the Dionysian impulse. If allowed to run wild, the devastating effects are well documented in myth and in reality. If moderated, the Dionysian attributes combined with honest self-reflection and natural empathy can lead to wisdom. Perhaps this is why Athena, the Goddess of Wisdom, is said to have retrieved the heart of Dionysos (in the Orphic mysteries), and brought him back to life.

Ariadne and the Contemporary Woman

An Ariadne woman is attracted to men who embody Dionysian attributes. Depending on her consciousness and strength of ego, she will gravitate towards either the positive or less-evolved aspects. She might be attracted to a priest, or any sort of spiritual or psychological guide (all who mediate between the visible and invisible worlds); or conversely a murderer with Dionysian attributes. Mystics, poets, artists, cult leaders, addicts, and murderers all fall under the Dionysian rubric.

She finds herself with men who have a tendency towards extremity of mood (i.e., bipolarity, or fluctuation of identity from charm to rage). "Major emotional shifts are precipitated by minimal events."[209] In relationship with a man like this, the Ariadne woman is subject to the Dionysian experience of agony and ecstasy on a regular basis.

"...go to him, stay with him if you can, but be prepared to bleed..." The lyrics of Joni Mitchell's *A Case of You*, Blue Album (1971) qualifies as the theme song of the Ariadne woman until she finds redemption by integrating her Dionysian *animus*.

The Ariadne woman is drawn to the depths as well as to transcendent states of consciousness, and is never quite at home in the ordinary world and its day-to-day concerns. She is not afraid to surrender to altered states of consciousness. In keeping with her

---

[209] Shinoda Bolen, *Gods in Everyman*, p. 259.

capacity to surrender, the Ariadne woman likes to dance. The Cretan architect and craftsman, Daedalus, is said to have not only designed the labyrinth but also a dancing ground especially for Ariadne.[210]

Ariadne women love, and are at home on and near the water. Walter F. Otto, respected philologist and religious historian, writes,

> Ariadne, herself, is the woman of the sea, at home on the islands, carried away over the sea by the son of Poseidon, Theseus, and taken up by Dionysus into his band like the women of the islands, who are said to have followed him to Argos and were known by the name of sea women.[211]

We might also interpret this as a woman who is comfortable with the depths of consciousness.

The Ariadne woman often has had a controlling, if not despotic, father prone to rage and harboring secrets. Remember Ariadne's father, King Minos, and the Minotaur he had hidden under the palace. I would venture to offer that most women suffer forms of patriarchal despotism at some point in their lives in view of the imbalance of our culture. The Ariadne woman gains courage and inner strength by liberating herself from the despotic, brutish *animus* in fathers and in lovers. Once she integrates her Dionysian *animus*, she will not suffer bullies or bullying from a man (Minotaur behavior), or be prone to victimization in a patriarchal culture.

The Ariadne woman has the courage to free herself from soul-strangling situations, even at tremendous price, and will never be happy with a man who lacks courage, or in a situation that is subjugating or silencing her. The Ariadne woman craves the freedom to be herself and "to follow her own drummer."

---

[210] W. F. Otto, *Dionysus,* p. 186.

[211] Otto, *Dionysus,* p. 182.

Goddesses in the Ariadne Woman

The Ariadne woman carries attributes of several goddesses. Her ability to incisively extricate herself from unwanted situations and to strategize is an *Athena* trait.[212]

> The martial and domestic skills associated with Athena involve planning and execution, activities that require purposeful thinking.[213]

Remember, Ariadne gives Theseus the plan and the weapon to overcome the Minotaur deep within the labyrinth. In fact, she possesses a needed trait that purely Dionysian males do *not* exhibit in their focus on the intensity of the present, making her a positive partner for him.

She knows the Underworld, like Dionysos' first mother in the Orphic myth, *Persephone*. What does it mean to have familiarity with the Underworld?

> Symbolically, the Underworld can represent deeper layers of the psyche, a place where memories and feelings have been "buried" (the personal unconscious) and where images, patterns, instincts, and feelings that are archetypal and shared by humanity are found (the collective unconscious). When these areas are explored in analysis, underground images are produced in dreams. The dreamer may be in a basement, often with many corridors and rooms like *labyrinths*...Persephone, the Queen and Guide of the Underworld, represents the ability to move back and forth between the ego-based reality of the "real"

---

212 J. Shinoda Bolen, *Goddesses in Everywoman*, p. 78.
213 Shinoda Bolen, *Goddesses in Everywoman*, p. 76.

world and the unconscious or archetypal reality of the psyche.[214]

Ariadne possesses these *Persephone* skills. She has experience with the darker side of humanity. Though there is a certain enduring innocence to her, she is not naïve. Persephone was abducted and raped by Hades, the god of the Underworld, and forced to live in that realm until her mother, Demeter, wins her freedom from Zeus. Yet, by that time, she seems to have found a place in the realm of the Shades, as its queen, and never abandons it entirely despite her yearly visits to the land of the living. Ariadne, like Persephone, has knowledge of the Underworld and its misshapen and suffering inhabitants (*e.g.* the Minotaur). Kerényi writes that offerings were made to Ariadne as a "*subterranean goddess*" at Argos.[215]

We might also translate the Underworld as the underbelly of society, or the shadowed realms of consciousness and the deepest layers of the unconscious.

> When the Persephone archetype is active, it is possible for a woman to mediate between the two levels and to integrate both into her personality. She may also serve as a guide for others who "visit" the Underworld in their dreams and fantasies, or may help those who are "abducted" and who lose touch with reality.[216]

The Ariadne woman, like Persephone, can make a good detective, forensic pathologist, anthropologist and researcher, or depth psychologist. She has the courage to face what may be lurking in the shadows of life and of consciousness.

---

[214] Shinoda Bolen, *Goddesses in Everywoman*, pp. 202, 203. Italics mine for emphasis.

[215] C. Kerényi, *Dionysos*, p. 103.

[216] Shinoda Bolen, *Goddesses in Everywoman*, p. 203.

Like Persephone, she has experienced betrayal, but rather than abduction, she suffers on account of abandonment. Abandonment throws her into a withering-away, "failure to thrive" version of depression, symbolized by the hanging motif in the Ariadne myth. However, having survived this initiation, and triumphed, she achieves the crown of a realized *Self*.

Ariadne's crown was supposed to have been fashioned by the craftsman god Hephaestus, and retrieved from the sea, where it had lain in the depths.[217] She has won the crown as a result of her own journey into the depths. The crown, being a circle, is a symbol of the all-inclusive *Self*, as Jung defines it. If an Ariadne woman survives that journey, she has the possibility of renewal and wholeness/holiness. Ariadne, the "Holy One,"[218] becomes the "Utterly Clear,"[219] that is, unblemished and transparent to the light of the *Self*. Ariadne's wholeness, imaged as a circle of stars, finding its home in the heavens, the Corona Borealis, represents her transformation. From this transcendent perspective born of life, death, and rebirth, Ariadne is qualified to act as a guide for souls traversing the depths and seeking the heights.

Finally, the golden glow of Aphrodite, goddess of love, gently illuminates the psyche of the Ariadne woman. Ariadne was worshipped as *Ariadne Aphrodite* on the island of Cyprus.[220]

> With Ariadne the nature of the Dionysiac woman is exalted to marvelous heights. She is the perfect image of the beauty which, when it is touched by its lover, gives life immortality.[221]

---

[217] W.F. Otto, *Dionysus*, p. 182.
[218] R. Graves, *The White Goddess*, p. 99.
[219] C. Keréenyi, *Dionysos*, p. 104.
[220] Otto, *Dionysus*, p. 182.
[221] Otto, *Dionysus*, p. 181.

A woman with Aphrodite gifts may not be physically more attractive than other women and she may even appear quite plain. But she naturally possesses a magnetism that draws others to her, if she has not intentionally repressed those powers in reaction to an environment that makes their expression unsafe.

Jungian analyst Jean Shinoda Bolen calls Aphrodite the "Alchemical Goddess," and her special state of consciousness "Aphrodite Consciousness."[222] Aphrodite has the gift of creating beauty wherever she is, and of finding beauty in those upon whom she focuses the light of her attention, drawing forth "gold" from someone with whom she comes into contact and who may seem quite ordinary. A woman, graced by Aphrodite, has the ability to bring out the sparkling talent and virtues of people with whom she comes into intimate, not necessarily romantic, contact, even in passing (perhaps even through a sweet smile directed towards the box boy at the grocery store).

> Aphrodite consciousness is neither like a living room lamp that illuminates everything with the radius of its glow with a warm, soft light, nor like a spotlight or laser beam. I think of Aphrodite consciousness as analogous to theater lighting (*quite appropriate considering our topic*)[223] that illuminates a stage. What we behold in this limelight enhances, dramatizes, or magnifies the impact...this special lighting helps us to be emotionally transported...In turn, those onstage can become in-spired...energized by the rapport they sense being directed towards them.[224]

---

[222] J. Shinoda Bolen, *Goddesses in Everywoman*, p. 224-227.

[223] Parenthesis mine.

[224] Shinoda Bolen, *Goddesses in Everywoman,* p. 226.

Her enthusiastic reception of another's dreams and goals helps their realization. Shinoda Bolen calls her a "vision carrier" in this capacity. Because Aphrodite sees the best in another, and draws it forward, the other is inclined to meet her vision. She does this for lovers, friends, children, and therapeutic clients if she happens to be a psychologist. Ariadne was a "vision carrier" for Theseus, believing in him and assisting him at great risk to herself, having secretly defied her father, the king. Surely, Ariadne was blessed with the magnetism Aphrodite can bestow if she was able to win the love of the most sensually attuned god, Dionysos, even in her sleep.

Aphrodite's deep sensual appreciation of another evokes Dionysian pleasure and further links her with Ariadne:

> Such a woman takes in people in the same way that a wine connoisseur attends to, and notices the characteristics of, an interesting new wine. To appreciate the metaphor fully, imagine a wine buff enjoying the pleasure of getting acquainted with an unknown wine. She (or he) holds the goblet up to the light to note the color and clarity of the wine. She inhales the bouquet, and takes a lingering sip to capture the character and smoothness of the wine; she even savors the aftertaste...Basking in the glow of her focus, (others) feel attractive and interesting as she actively draws them out and reacts in a loving and affirming way.[225]

Ariadne, like Aphrodite, is able to take risks, live fully in the moment, give all for love, and create something new: a new life and a new way of being with new possibility. She and Dionysos were said to have had many children. An Ariadne woman's children can be babies or wonderful new projects—from works of art, design, and literature,

---

[225] Shinoda Bolen, *Goddesses in Everywoman*, p. 227.

to philosophic and scientific breakthroughs. Two thoughts can merge, a spark occur, and a new idea is born. Aphrodite is she who creates the electric attraction needed for the spark. It is she who engenders "chemistry" in a relationship whether it be a romantic, platonic or a creative partnership. And it is she who creates the environment necessary for the alchemy of psychological and spiritual transformation. The soul is irrevocably transformed as a result of her touch. Aphrodite graces the Ariadne woman with possibility and high destiny.

As Ariadne was a model for a number of Roman women involved in initiation and even earlier for many Greek women, perhaps there is an Ariadne even in women who appear to resonate to other archetypes but are interested in *Individuation.*

13

CONCLUSION

We are coming into something completely new: a new
femininity balanced by a new masculinity. The Goddess
is coming to light. She is coming through the Earth and
through our physical bodies, but we have to relate to her
with our own individual consciousness. Otherwise we
could be sucked back into unconscious matriarchy…[226]

Ariadne's story illustrates the possibility of *conscious* femininity,
not a return to unconscious matriarchy, or stagnation in a disconnected
and oppressive patriarchy. Paradoxically, the ancient myths are keys to
navigating the seas of psyche, no matter when, or where, we find
ourselves. Though the myths emerged in the distant past, the archetypes
that people them are timeless.

The gods and goddesses and their stories emerged during an
epoch in which humanity had very real experiences of the forces of
nature, and sensed invisible presences. The personification of those
forces into named Beings (the goddesses and gods) was a sort of
technology designed to help humanity interact with realms and
energies they *felt* and intuited far more clearly than we have for a very
long time. In the pursuit of reason, consciousness, and individuality,
that proximity to an intimate relationship with nature and the unseen
has faded. However, it is only through once again cultivating awareness

[226] M. Woodman, *Conscious Femininity*, p. 19.

and sensitivity to nature, to shared being, as well as to the invisible threads between us, the world, and the cosmos, that we can survive and move forward. Arising from the deeper strata of consciousness, these stories contain indications which can guide us into what Marion Woodman describes as "new territory."

We are undoubtedly "coming into something completely new." The unparalleled discoveries in science, especially in physics and astrophysics, as well as developments in technology, have irrevocably changed our perception of our home planet, our Universe, and our place in it. Simultaneously, ancient texts and civilizations long buried have reemerged, shifting our perceptions of our most inviolate beliefs.[227] Old forms and structures are breaking down on all fronts. In tandem with these breakthroughs and revelations, we have contrived sure methods of self-destruction and are running behind in meeting the responsibility and maturity required to possess such power.

The time calls for a leap in consciousness. We must truly grow up if we are to survive. That leap includes reflective *self*-awareness, empathy, and finding ways to celebrate our differences even while we honor our common humanity. It requires a realization that "Nature is our home, and in nature we are *at* home."[228]

This writing has been an excursion into the path of *Integration* and *Individuation* through the heart, available especially to women. As the masculine is so integral a part of that path to feminine wholeness, a new masculinity, which reembraces the relational values and creative passion demonstrated by Dionysos, necessarily plays an integral part of the journey. This exploration has hoped to offer not only a model of *Integration* of a supportive *animus* for women, but also a reclaiming of the embodied creative, relational, erotic and passionate masculinity available to men.

---

[227] An example is the discovery of the Nag Hammadi scriptures in 1945, which give us alternate readings of the story of Christ, buried at least since the fourth century A.D. and thought to have been composed in the first or second century after Christ. The discovery of the Dead Sea Scrolls in 1947 is another.

[228] C. Rovelli, *Seven Brief Lessons on Physics*, p. 79.

Our journey has led us on a voyage of discovery through India, Egypt, and Crete, to the flowering of his celebrations and mysteries in Classical Greece, and finally to the intimate expression of his deep mysteries available to women in Roman times, unearthed in the discovery of the Villa of Mysteries in Pompeii. We have seen how his worship was always particularly valued by, and valuable to, women. We have learned the stories associated with the Dionysian current and especially delved into the meaningful symbolism of the *coniunctio*, or *sacred marriage* of Ariadne and Dionysos.

Our exploration of the "light" (conscious) and "shadow" (unconscious), as well as the *solar* and *chthonic* expressions of sacred masculine and feminine, has revealed a long-standing emphasis on conscious *solar* patriarchal values and a concomitant suppression of the more relational, earth-honoring perspectives. "Power over" has run its course and there is an urgent need to shift to share cooperative empowerment, a value expressed in the ancient symbolism of Dionysos and the Great Mother, as well as in the story of the Ariadne and Dionysos. Marion Woodman's teaching that we are at the threshold of entering an entirely new phase of consciousness, which she has called *Conscious Femininity*, finds an archetypal foundation in the myth of the marriage of Ariadne and Dionysos.

Dionysos and Ariadne are emblematic of the goal of personal *Individuation* for women, in that Ariadne has the courage to break through all repressive forms of patriarchy, not only overcoming the distortions of the unconscious represented by the Minotaur lurking in the psychic depths but also risking all for what her heart tells her is true. Dionysos, as her true partner, is a virile masculinity who knows, supports, and deeply honors the feminine. He sparks her and makes her fecund. She experiences her vital creativity in relationship with him.

Dionysos is a fitting archetype for what could heal the wounded masculine. He does not lose his masculinity even as he transcends boundaries but is able to comfortably merge and celebrate surrender. He is an image of the masculine that has profound reverence for life and honors the expression of its power within his own body, while continuing to revere a partner who will receive him. That partner could be a human other, or the Earth herself, in relationship with him.

At the core of this study is Love and Freedom, the love that brings us together with one another and the Earth and the freedom to uniquely express ourselves. It is love that does not bind but weaves together, and that heals us. This weaving, if it be true love, does not possess, suffocate, or suppress. True love celebrates individuality and supports uniqueness while joining *with* the other. Dionysian values are first and foremost freedom, naturalness, as well as transcendent consciousness, and that which bridges all separation, Love. It is hoped that this study offers insight into the wisdom dwelling within the archetypes and stories of Dionysos and Ariadne, leading to a deepening in consciousness and further progress on the human journey towards wholeness.

I close with a prayer written by the contemporary devotee of Dionysos, H. Jeremiah Lewis:

Dionysos, make me drunk on the wine of life!
Open me up to every experience
so that when it is time to stand before the judges in the West
I will be able to say that I wasted not a second of my life
and that I ended my days without a single regret.
Cause my spirit to overflow its bounds,
like the Nile spilling over its banks,
and may this inundation make the soil fertile
so that every type of crop and plant take root in it.
Dionysos, nurture the seed that I plant and guide it until it reaches fruition.
Be just as gentle to me, Lord, as I undergo the journey into wholeness.
Show me the source of true being,
which survives transformation,
even that of death,
so that I might see
just how small and powerless my fears are.[229]
Io Evohe![230]

---

[229] H.J. Lewis, *Ecstatic*, p. 376.

[230] "Io Evohe" is a rendering of the cry invoking Dionysos in ancient Greece.

THE VILLA
OF MYSTERIES

THE FIRST SCENE

Scala / Art Resources NY

THE SECOND AND THIRD SCENES

Scala / Art Resources NY

THE THIRD AND FOURTH SCENES

Scala / Art Resources NY

THE FIFTH, SIXTH, AND SEVENTH SCENES

Scala / Art Resources NY

THE SEVENTH AND EIGHTH SCENES

Scala / Art Resources NY

THE NINTH SCENE

THE TENTH SCENE

Scala / Art Resources NY

Bibliography

Abraham, L. *A Dictionary of Alchemical Imagery,* Cambridge, Cambridge University Press, 1998.

Allen, R. H. *Star Names:, Their Lore and Meaning.* (First published by G.E. Stechert in 1899), republished in Mineola, Dover Publications, 1963.

Apollodorus, (Robin Hard, Trans. and notes), *The Library of Greek Mythology,* New York, Oxford University Press, 1997.

Aromatico, A. *Alchemy: The Great Secret,* New York, Harry N. Abrams, 2000.

Bachofen, J.J. (Ralph Manheim, Trans.). *Myth, Religion and Mother Right,* Princeton, Princeton University Press, 1967.

Bleakley, A. *Fruits of the Moon Tree:, The Medicine Wheel and Transpersonal Psychology,* Gateway Books, 1984.

Bolen, Jean Shinoda. *Gods in Everyman.* San Francisco, Harper & Row, 1989.

_____. *Goddesses in Everywoman.* San Francisco, Harper & Row, 1984.

Bradway, K. *Villa of Mysteries:, Pompeii Initiation Rites of Women,* booklet published by C.G. Jung Institute of San Francisco, 1982.

Bramshaw, V. *Dionysos:, Exciter to Frenzy.* London, Avalonia Books, 2013.

Cosmopoulos, M.B. *Greek Mysteries: The Archaeology of Ancient Greek Secret Cults,* London, Routledge Publishing, 2003.

Claremont de Castillejo, I. *Knowing Woman,* New York, G.P. Putnam's Sons, 1973.

Daniélou, A. *Shiva and Dionysus.* London, East-West Publications Ltd., 1982.

_____. *Gods of Love and Ecstasy: The Traditions of Shiva and Dionysus.* New York, Inner Traditions International, 1984.

Downing, C. *The Goddess: Mythological Images of the Feminine,* New York, Crossroad Publishing, 1981.

Edmond, R.G. (Ed.), *The "Orphic" Gold Tablets and the Greek Religion: Further Along the Path.* Cambridge, Cambridge University Press, 2011.

Euripides. *Bacchae,* (Dodds, E.R. Ed.), Oxford, Clarendon Press, 1960.

Evans, Arthur. *The God of Ecstasy: Sex-Roles and the Madness of Dionysos.* London, St. Martin's Press, 1988.

Fierz-David, Linda. *Women's Dionysian Initiation, The Villa of Mysteries in Pompeii* (Trans. Gladys Phelan), Dallas, Spring Publications, 1988.

Fierz-David, Linda; Hall, Nor. *Dreaming in Red, The Women's Dionysian Initiation Chamber in Pompeii,* Putnam, Spring Publications, 2005.

Georgieff, Stephanie. *The Black Madonna: Mysterious Soul Companion.* Denver, Outskirts Press, 2016.

Gimbutas, Marija. *The Prehistory of Eastern Europe, Part 1.* Cambridge, Peabody Museum at Harvard University, 1956.

Graves, Robert. *The White Goddess: A Historical Grammar of Poetic Myth,* New York, Farrar, Straus and Giroux, 1948.

Guthrie, W.K.C. *Orpheus and Greek Religion,* First published: London, *Methuen, 1952,* republished, Princeton, Princeton University Press, 1993.

Haeffner, Mark, *The Dictionary of Alchemy: From Maria Prophetissa to Isaac Newton,* London, The Aquarian Press, 1991.

Herberger, Charles, *The Thread of Ariadne: The Labyrinth of the Calendar of Minos,* New York, Philosophical Library, 1972.

Hall, Nor. *Those Women.* Published in *Dreaming in Red.* Putnam, Connecticut, Spring Publishing, 2005.

Hamilton, Edith. *Mythology.* London, Penguin Publishing, 1953.

Harding, M. Esther. Introduction. *Dreaming in Red,* Linda Fierz-David, Nor Hall. Putnam, Spring Publications, 2005.

The Herder Symbol Dictionary, (Trans. Boris Matthews), Asheville, Chiron Publishing, revised edition, 1996.

Heschel, Susannah. *On Being a Jewish Feminist.* New York, Schocken, 1995.

Hickey, Isabel. *Astrology: a Cosmic Science.* Waltham, New Pathways, 1970.

Hillman, James. *The Feeling Function.* In M.L. von Franz, J. Hillman *Jung's Typology.* Dallas, Spring Publications, 1971.

_____. *The Myth of Analysis.* New York, Harper & Row, 1972.

_____. *Re-visioning Psychology.* New York, Harper & Row, 1975.

_____. *The Puer Papers.* Dallas, Spring Publishing, 1979.

Hollis, James. *The Middle Passage: From Misery to Meaning in Midlife.* Toronto, Inner City Books, 1993.

Jobes, Gertrude. *Dictionary of Mythology: Folklore and Symbols, Parts 1 & 2.* New York, The Scarecrow Press, 1962.

Johnson, Robert. *Ecstasy.* San Francisco, Harper & Row, 1987.

Jung, Carl. *Psychology and Alchemy* (CW Vol. 12). Bollingen Series XX, Princeton, Princeton University Press, 1953, second edition 1968.

_____. *Mysterium Coniunctionis* (CW Vol. 14). Bollingen Series XX, Princeton, Princeton University Press, 1963, second edition, 1970.

_____. *Psychological Types* (CW Vol. 6). Bollingen Series XX, Princeton, Princeton University Press, 1971, second edition, 1976.

Jung, Emma. *Animus and Anima.* Dallas, Spring Publishing, 1987.

Kaltsas, Nikolaos and Shapiro, Alan (Eds.). *Worshipping Women: Ritual and Reality in Ancient Athens.* New York, Alexander S. Onassis Public Benefit Foundation in collaboration with the National Archaeological Museum, Athens, 2008.

Kast, Verena. *The Nature of Loving* (Trans. B. Matthews). Willamette, Chiron Publications, 1984.

Kerényi, Carl. *Prometheus, Archetypal Image of Human Existence.* (Trans. R. Manheim), Princeton, Princeton University Press, 1963.

_____.*Dionysos: Archetypal Image of Indestructible Life.* (Trans. R. Manheim)
Princeton, Princeton University Press, 1976.

Koltuv, Barbara. *The Book of Lilith.* York Beach: Nicholas-Hays Inc., 1986.

Lemming, David Adams. *Oxford Companion of World Mythology.* Oxford, Oxford University Press, 2005.

Lewis, H. Jeremiah. *Ecstatic.* Nysa Press, 2011.

Lopez-Pedraza, Rafael, *Dionysus in Exile: On the Repression of the Body and Emotion.* Wilmette, Illinois, Chiron Publications, 2000.

Larousse World Mythology (Ed. Pierre Grimal*).* New York, Excalibur Books, 1981.

Luton, Frith. *Honey and the Hive.* Toronto, Inner City Books, 2011.

Maiuri, Amedeo. *La Villa Dei Misteri*, Istituto Poligrafico e Zecca Dello Stato, Libreria Dello Stato, 1967.

Matt, Daniel (Trans.). *The Zohar: Pritzker Edition, Vols. 1 & 2*, Redwood City, Stanford University Press, 2003.

Matthews, Caitlin. *Sophia, Goddess of Wisdom: The Divine Feminine from Black Goddess to World Soul*, London, Mandala, 1991.

Monaghan, Patricia. *The Book of Goddesses and Heroines.* New York, Plume Publications, 1981.

Monick, Eugene. *Phallos: Sacred Image of the Masculine.* Toronto, Inner City Books, 1987.

Morrissey, Michael P. *Consciousness and Transcendence. The Theology of Eric Voegelin.* Indiana, University of Notre Dame Press, 1994.

Nilsson, Martin P. *The Dionysiac Mysteries of the Hellenistic and Roman Age.* New York, Arno Press, 1975.

Otto, Walter F. *Dionysus: Myth and Cult.* Indiana, Indiana University Press, 1965.

Ovid, *The Metamorphoses of Ovid*. (Trans. Allen Mandelbaum), New York, Harcourt, 1993.

Paris, Ginette, (Trans. Joanna Mott). *Pagan Grace, Dionysos, Hermes, and Goddess Memory in Daily Life*. Spring Publications, Putnam, Connecticut, Spring Publishing, 1990, 2003.

Pearson, Carol S. *Persephone Rising*, New York, Harper Elixer, 2015.

_____. *The Hero Within*, New York, Harper Elixer, 2015.

_____. *Awakening the Hero Within*, New York, Harper Elixer, 2015.

Pike, Albert. *Morals and Dogma of the Ancient and Accepted Scottish Rite of Freemasonry*, Washington D.C., The Supreme Council of the Southern Jurisdiciton, A.A.S.R., U.S.A., 1871, revised 1950.

Qualls-Corbett, Nancy. *The Sacred Prostitute*. Toronto, Inner City Books, 1988.

Rovelli, Carlo. *Seven Brief Lessons on Physics*, New York, Riverbed Books, 2014.

Samuels, Andrew; Shorter, Bani; Plaut, Fred. *A Critical Dictionary of Jungian Analysis*. New York, Routledge & Kegan Paul, in association with Methuen, 1986.

Shlain, Leonard. *The Alphabet Versus the Goddess: The Conflict Between Word and Image*. New York, Penguin House, 1999.

Sjoo, Monica and Mor, Barbara. *The Great Cosmic Mother: Rediscovering the Religion of the Earth*. San Francisco, Harper & Row, 1987.

Spiegelman, J. Marvin. *Notes for the Underground*. Spring Magazine, Dallas, Spring Publications, 1970.

Steiner, Rudolf. *Freedom and the Catholic Church*, Lecture III of III, Dornach, June 6, 1920. Rudolf Steiner Archive and e. Lib.

Taylor, Thomas (Trans.). *The Hymns of Orpheus*. London, Forgotten Books, 2007.

Time Magazine, October 15, 1956. *Science: Man of Pompeii*.

Tresidder, Jack, (Gen. Editor), *The Complete Dictionary of Symbols,* San Francisco, Chronicle Books, 2004.

Walker, Barbara G. *The Woman's Dictionary of Symbols and Sacred Objects*, San Francisco, Harper & Row, 1988.

Walker, Alice. *In Search of Our Mothers' Garden: Womanist Prose*, Boston, Mariner Books, 2003.

Walker, Rebecca. Ms. Magazine, *Becoming the Third Wave,* 1992.

West, Melissa Gayle, *Exploring the Labyrinth: A Guide for Healing and Spiritual Growth*, New York, Broadway Books, 2000.

Wheelwright, Jane H. *Women and Men.* San Francisco, C.G. Jung Institute, 1977.

Whitmont, Edward. *The Symbolic Quest.* Princeton, Princeton University Press, 1978.

Woodman, Marion. *Conscious Femininity: Interviews with Marion Woodman.* Toronto, Inner City Books, 1993.

Young Eisendrath, Polly. *Hags and Heroes: a Feminist Approach to Jungian Psychotherapy with Couples.* Toronto, Inner City Books, 1984.

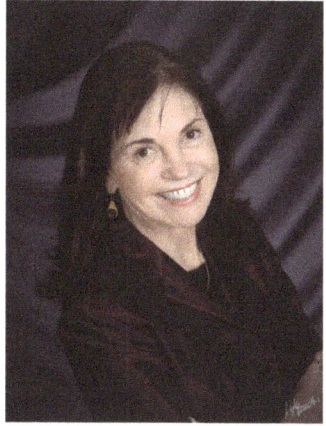

ABOUT THE AUTHOR

A. Marina Aguilar, M.A., received her Masters in Counseling Psychology at Pacifica Graduate Institute, Santa Barbara and has been a practicing depth psychotherapist and educator since 1990. She specializes in and has taught mythology, comparative religion, and the Western mystery teachings including Kabbalah and Spiritual Alchemy. Having lived in the United States, Mexico, and Europe, her work bridges cultures, continents, and spiritual modalities and focuses on increasing consciousness and wholeness.